I0803832

THE PURITAN ICE COMPANIES

THE ICE EMPIRE OF CALIFORNIA'S CENTRAL COAST

DAVID PETRY

THE History PRESS

Puritan Ice, Santa Barbara, plant #1, circa 1923. *Connie Phillips collection.*

Published by The History Press
Charleston, SC 29403
www.historypress.net

First published 2012

Manufactured in the United States

ISBN 978.1.60949.877.1

Library of Congress CIP data applied for.

To John Fritsche

Contents

Introduction

The fifty years from 1895 through 1945 could be called the Great American Ice Age. During these years, ice reinvented our railroads, reinvented our food, reinvented our economy and reinvented even our communities. In 1895, more people lived within five miles of a farm than not. Only a small percentage of food traveled beyond twenty miles, a long day's travel with a horse and cart. The food that did travel, like potatoes and corn, was hardy and needed no cooling. Or it was livestock on the hoof, expensive, difficult and very inefficient.

By 1945, America was a different place. Instead of people spread like butter over the farmland and fledgling cities, now the cities boomed and drained the farmlands of people. Food—much more food than could have been imagined fifty years earlier—traveled, and it routinely traveled thousands of miles.

Ice was the medium that allowed so many changes to occur in such a short time frame.

The massive change, when it came down to it, was a simple distribution problem. How could Americans grow, package, move, distribute, store and market fresh foods to get them to the places where the population was moving? The answer seemed simple as well.

Logically, closing the gulf between rural grower and city grocer was a problem the grower or grocer would naturally want to solve. But put anything in place—a proposition, an idea, a business—and it will only roll downhill if the underlying conditions are right. For the grower-to-

Ice hooks, Puritan Ice, Guadalupe plant #2, 2010. *Photo by David Petry.*

grocer problem, the distances were too great, the costs too high and the risks too real.

The growers were dispersed, unorganized, small and undercapitalized. The grocers of 1895 were in the same boat. And food was not like steel; profit margins were far too small to bear the cost of a national infrastructure. It was only through the Great American Ice Age that parties on both ends of the line created cooperatives, consolidated and merged and began to form regional and even national companies.

But at the beginning, it was the rail companies that found it in their best interests to step up. They created and then heavily optimized the infrastructure to make it work. One of the central requirements of the infrastructure was ice to keep the produce cool. It was the rail companies that developed and built rail cars with ice bunkers. And in many cases, it was the rail companies that manufactured the ice at hundreds of plants along the way.

The rail and ice industries quickly consolidated and were run by regional monopolies. There were start-ups, but the small rail and ice companies were either bought out or priced out of existence. Capital in the massive rail and ice firms moved like tides; prices could drop or contracts dry up, and independent firms all too often found themselves with expensive, brand-new plants and no market.

One of the very few local ice companies that escaped this fate was Puritan Ice of Santa Barbara, operating from 1922 to 1986. Somehow the founders obtained insider knowledge and privilege in order to not just be in the right place at the right time but also to gain and maintain a permanent immunity, even when the company bumped up against giants like Union Ice of San Francisco.

An unaccountable anachronism in the ice world, Puritan was a company that reflected and embodied the larger trends and developments in the country.

Puritan Ice was central in the creation of food development, both produce and poultry. Almost single-handedly, Puritan created or significantly expanded the agricultural markets for Guadalupe, Santa Maria, Lompoc, Atascadero, Oxnard and Blythe. In the course of the company's trajectory, it helped establish the Japanese growers in the Santa Maria Valley and then supplanted them with Mexican braceros during World War II. Puritan developed the largest egg and poultry farm on earth in Atascadero. It fought for and won the domestic ice business in Santa Barbara, Lompoc and Guadalupe. The company went to Blythe, California, where it more than doubled agricultural production in the valley and served the ice needs of General Patton's Desert Training Center.

Exterior, Puritan Ice, Guadalupe plant #2, 2010. *Photo by David Petry.*

Puritan then transformed itself in the face of the advent of frozen foods and mechanically refrigerated trucks. The company introduced vacuum pre-cooling—a process by which produce was chilled prior to loading—and the addition of blowers to fill loaded rail cars and trucks with crushed ice.

But soon the ice business was melting away. Puritan diversified into feedlots, equipment leasing and distribution, specifically of Pepsi-Cola. With a few of the ice plants still in operation, the leasing firm took on clients like Motel 6 and Sambo's and, riding on the coattails of these companies' successes, grew to open leasing offices in eighteen states.

The company is fascinating for all these reasons and more. How this underdog was able to find a toehold among successful monopolies, not just once but several times, is a story unto itself. How it straddled the Great Depression, rode out World War II and then ascended through the super-heated times of the 1960s and '70s like a rocket are all interesting facets of a unique and agile company. Even the company's demise in 1986 was on a high note.

Yet the ice industry in Santa Barbara was nearly invisible. The Puritan Ice plant stood a half block from the beach, at 325 East Cabrillo Boulevard. Though it produced fifty tons of ice daily, most residents in town never noticed the building, much less knew what was done inside. The plant was shielded by a row of trees, and the building was a utilitarian cluster of white rectangles.

Invisible or not, Puritan Ice was a linchpin to history. Located in Santa Barbara, it connected California's northern Central Coast to the south and connected this region of California to the eastern United States. To understand Puritan is to understand a critical moment in both human and regional history.

Chapter 1

Ice on the California Riviera

Some Santa Barbarans remember the red-and-white delivery trucks for the local ice company, emblazoned with "Puritan Ice—Be Perspicacious!" For several decades, ice deliverymen stopped at the back of every dining and grocery establishment and then drove their trucks out of the downtown corridor and delivered ice to every neighborhood in town.[1]

Downtown, the drivers pulled up at the back door of a restaurant or bar and read the ice order—a sign mounted on the wall or door with a single nail in the center. The owner would spin the sign: three hundred, two hundred, one hundred or fifty pounds. Whatever weight was pointed upward was the order to fill. At the back of the ice wagon or truck, the drivers would haul a fresh block of ice to the tailgate and, using the lines scored into the ice block back at the plant, cut out chunks to fill the order. Then, with a snap of their ice tongs, they would shoulder the load and head through the door.

Cold storage units in these homes and restaurants were sometimes called refrigerators in the early days, but mostly they were just iceboxes, insulated cabinets with one or two doors on the front and an open compartment on top for ice. Heat inside the compartment traveled up to where it met the ice-cold roof of the compartment, condensed to water and slipped down the walls to the drains. For most businesses, the ice was filled daily. The amount depended on how much perishable product the business kept on hand.

When the trucks turned off State Street and headed out to homes, the signs on the back doors had smaller numbers—one hundred, seventy-five,

Jeff Ray of John Ray and Sons, Troy, New York, carrying ice, circa 1920. *John Ray and Sons.*

Residential ice delivery sign.

fifty, twenty-five—the homeowner spinning the desired quantity to the top position. The home iceboxes were smaller than the commercial ones. Residences had a two- or three-times-a-week delivery schedule, and the deliverymen were sometimes given keys to the back doors of homes so they could let themselves in.

Their role in each household could be a bit different. In some, they simply delivered, sliding the new ice in next to the old and marking the quantity on their clipboards for accounting back at the plant. In others, they might clean out the melt tray at the bottom of the icebox, check the drain lines and clean the ice tray itself. Every six months or so, they might check the food compartment door seals and talk with the residents about the new iceboxes, the ones with painted steel sides in pastel shades, or with the icebox embedded inside the refrigerated compartment or, best of all, a bigger icebox. Iceboxes and ice delivery were creating a demand for perishable food in our diets and homes, and over the early years of ice availability, the market began to generate new options for perishable foods. It all needed someplace to go. Where better than into a bigger icebox in every kitchen?

In 1922, when Puritan Ice opened in Santa Barbara, there were two ice delivery companies in town already: Santa Barbara Ice and Ord Ice. But that's not where Puritan first focused. It came to fulfill a demand to cool commercial produce on the way to distant markets. To hear the well-worn anecdotes from family, ex-employees and journalists, the fact that Puritan chose Santa Barbara was almost serendipitous.

LIKELY STORY

In a brief company history published in 1972, the author reported, "The first venture of the Phillips-Dalzell team was the Puritan Ice Company, located in Santa Barbara, California. The location was chosen because the partners wanted to work and live in a seaport city. Subsequent Ice Plants were constructed in Guadalupe, Lompoc, Atascadero, and Blythe, California."[2]

According to a story related ten years earlier by Don Phillips, founder L.R. Phillips's second son, for an article celebrating forty years of operations, "One night my father and mother [visiting from Los Angeles] went up to the El Encanto for dinner. After enjoying that view, it took little effort on their part to convince Mr. Dalzell that Santa Barbara was the place to locate."[3]

Less than a year later, in 1922, the Phillipses were back, living in a rental at 1111 Nopal Street, a half mile from the El Encanto. They were expecting their first child and launching the new firm. T.P. Dalzell and his wife, Sara, moved to the area a few short weeks later and took up residence two doors down, at 1121 Nopal.

The El Encanto story carries the unquestioned weight of an old family tradition. It has in its cozy threads the frontier spirit of stepping into the unknown, the raw talent of cunning men shaping something from nothing and the innocence of good men trying to do good things.

But the story is unlikely.

By 1922, ice was big business in California, whether it was for home delivery or rail icing. The Southern Pacific's subsidiary, Pacific Fruit Express (PFE), ran most of the rail icing plants in California, and where it did not, the plants were operated under contracts with PFE. PFE controlled the ice business. The largest contractor, cornering the majority of the ice delivery business in California and holding down several corners of the rail car icing business as well, was San Francisco–based Union Ice.

Who were Phillips and Dalzell? How did they win a contract from PFE? How did they get their foot into a door big enough to crush scores of other up-and-coming companies already?

For one thing, they had a benefactor. Constance Lowell, widow of astronomer Percival Lowell, fronted the two men as much as $250,000. This is according to family lore related by Leon Phillips's grandson, Bruce Phillips, but other accounts bear this out. The funds would have been enough to launch the company. But money was no guarantee of success in the ice business. Union Ice had a reputation for grinding up much larger, better-established concerns than upstarts like Phillips and Dalzell.

It could be that L.R. Phillips and T.P. Dalzell knew something the bigger players at the table did not. History was closing a door. Phillips and Dalzell found themselves looking squarely through the window that opened behind it.

The Ice Window

In 1922, to look at a map of California rail routes and ice plants, and understanding that you needed to top up the ice on high-value perishables in rail cars roughly every two to three hundred miles, you would see that perishable goods traveled north and south through the Central Valley of California. Plants churned out tons of ice daily in Oakland, Roseville, Turlock, Fresno, Tulare, Bakersfield and Los Angeles. A new ice plant in Salinas cooled the vegetables from local fields and sent them east to the main train lines. California's Central Coast, in terms of perishable goods, pretty much fended for itself. There were no markets big enough to attract rail service for produce.

In other words, any produce grown along the coast between Salinas and Los Angeles stayed where it was grown. It served local markets.

There were good reasons for this. Trains lived by passengers and freight. In 1920, in very general terms, the coast route carried mostly passengers, and the valley route carried mostly freight. Freight trains stayed in the valley because they followed routes that supplied freight at both ends and at points between. No one with a railroad company balance sheet on his desk wanted to see his freight cars hauling freight one way and sending empty cars back the other. The coast route was simply not developed enough to support freight runs. The run from Salinas to Paso Robles was sparsely populated—portions of it still are—and below Paso Robles the trains hit the Cuesta Grade. Coming south to Cuesta, it was a downhill breeze. Going north, however, the ten-mile grade climbed at nearly 7 percent, and if a train was hauling anything heavy, it slowed to a crawl.

The alignment of freight and passengers in Central and Southern California was dependent on the practices and policies of the rail companies involved. But a court decision known as the Santa Margarita Agreement was going to make a massive difference in a very specific market. And, though the agreement would not be reached until February 1923, this was the window that Phillips and Dalzell somehow knew about and stepped through in early 1922.[4]

The Santa Margarita Agreement arose out of machinations in the rail industry that reached every corner of the state of California and spilled past its boundaries for over twenty years before the decision was reached. There were many rail companies in California at the turn of the twentieth century, but there were just three that counted: the Southern Pacific, the Central Pacific and the Union Pacific. In 1899, the Central Pacific went through a reorganization to restructure its debt and shift ownership. As a result, it became a subsidiary of the larger Southern Pacific. Operating as a wholly owned separate entity, Central Pacific ran the route from Sacramento over the Sierra Nevadas and into the central western rail hub at Ogden, Utah.

The Southern Pacific Railroad owned over eight thousand miles of rail, stretching "from Portland, Oregon, south and southeast through southern California and Arizona, across Texas to New Orleans, along with its Overland Route across Nevada and Utah, to a connection with Union Pacific at Ogden."[5]

The primary competitor, Union Pacific, ran east from Portland, Oregon. On the way, it branched out into the wheat fields of eastern Washington, cut across Idaho and maintained critical lines into Montana and Utah. Then it cut across southern Wyoming and dropped into two parallel east–west lines that served Nebraska to the north and Kansas to the south. At Omaha and Kansas City, the lines exploded into a network of tracks that covered Iowa and northern Missouri.[6]

Edward Harriman owned the Union Pacific, but he wanted more. His rail lines snapped up crucial business delivering wheat and ores from the northwestern states and hauled livestock and passengers. But Harriman peered over the tops of the Sierras at the incredible bread (and fruit and vegetable) basket that California was becoming, not to mention the passenger destination it represented, and he rubbed his hands together (metaphorically) and schemed.

He approached Collis P. Huntington, president of the Southern Pacific, with purchase offers several times over the closing years of the nineteenth century, but Huntington was unmoved.

When Huntington died on August 13, 1900, Harriman watched the ensuing management disarray at the Southern Pacific for a few months and then stepped in with a decisive hand and bought Huntington's 46 percent of the company. In the climate of anti-corporate conglomeration of the times, Harriman explained that Union Pacific needed to control the larger Southern Pacific "to maintain and protect the position of the [Union Pacific] system and to safeguard its future against combinations of other lines." He admitted later, "We have bought not only a railroad, but an empire."[7]

The unification of the three largest rail lines in the western United States drew attention in Washington, D.C. Teddy Roosevelt was president, and he was personally invested in fighting the unfair business practices that seemed to be embodied in monopolies and trusts. Roosevelt's federal "trust-busters" descended and took Harriman into the courts. Harriman died in 1909, the case against his firm still pending. In 1912, in *United States v. Union Pacific* (226 US 61), Union Pacific was forced to divest itself of Southern Pacific.

In a separate 1922 case spawned by the earlier case, *United States v. Southern Pacific* (259 US 214), the Supreme Court directed Southern Pacific to terminate its control of the Central Pacific. Southern Pacific, however, took advantage of the fact that laws governing the Interstate Commerce Commission (ICC) had changed as of 1920, giving the ICC jurisdiction over railroads that controlled other railroads, and it re-presented its case, this time to the more favorably inclined ICC.

According to the Southern Pacific, echoing Harriman's earlier "required co-dependency" argument, the Southern Pacific and the Central Pacific railroads needed each other to fulfill freight obligations, and without the financial resources of the Southern Pacific, the Central Pacific would fail. In making the decision, the ICC tackled the question of the percentage of traffic that Southern Pacific was carrying across its longer and therefore more profitable (freight was billed by the mile) Sunset Route through

Southern California and east through Arizona. Figures showed that the Southern Pacific was in fact diverting a large percentage of California's freight "around the horn," so to speak, along its southernmost route, to garner higher freight charges.

The ICC decided to draw a line in the state and created the Santa Margarita Agreement, which required that all perishable freight traffic originating north of Santa Margarita, at the south end of California's Salinas Valley, would travel north and east by way of Ogden.

For most of America, and most of California, the decision was simply another wall made of paper that moved where the money was made from one locale to another, from one set of books to another, from one controlling entity to another. But there were some people who, while they probably had no idea the decision was even in the works, might have cared. They were Southern Californians.

In the big southern cities of California—Los Angeles and San Diego—populations were growing fast. By 1920, Los Angeles was the tenth-largest city in the United States, with a population of 576,673. Los Angeles County was just 68,000 short of 1 million.[8] San Diego was just 74,361; the county around it was 112,248, but the region was burgeoning.[9] However, this was a land of hot weather and scant water. It simply did not support growing fresh vegetables on a large scale, certainly not to the extent needed for over 1 million people.

Luckily, trainloads of fresh vegetables rolled in daily from the Salinas Valley.

But the Santa Margarita Agreement would close that door. Salinas Valley lettuce, carrots, tomatoes, cauliflower and broccoli would henceforth ship north and east. Pacific Fruit Express went about expanding what was already the largest ice manufacturing plant on the planet in Roseville, California. All that produce would need ice as it climbed the Sierras on its way to Omaha and St. Louis, Chicago, Boston and New York.

But where would the Los Angeles million get *their* produce?

The Icemen Cometh

Into this gap in service, even before the gap was created by law, stepped two men: Leon Redner Phillips and Ted Paul Dalzell.

L.R. Phillips was likely the "brains" of the operation. Born May 3, 1890, in Bath, in Stueben County, New York, his father was a dentist. The family had deep roots in the United States, arriving in Virginia in 1600, and like Virginia, the Phillips family was split during the Civil War. Leon's paternal grandfather was an officer for the Confederacy, while his maternal grandfather was a surgeon in the Union army.

Phillips grew up in New York and attended Cornell University, graduating in 1912 with a degree in mechanical engineering. At Cornell, he played on the varsity football team and rowed varsity crew. His interest in refrigeration was possibly sparked in school, as it was one of the emerging and exciting fields of the day. In any case, his first job took him to Chicago to the Swift & Company meatpacking firm.

Swift was at the forefront of rail shipment of packaged meats. Starting as a seller of cattle in the Boston region in 1855 and forming Swift & Company in Chicago in 1878, Gustavus Franklin Swift could see the future better than most. Swift began experimenting with shipping dressed beef by rail in the 1870s and quickly built a line of several thousand rail cars with ice bunkers.

Shipping livestock was highly inefficient. The stress on the animals was immense. On a cross-country trip, cows lost an average of 15 percent of their weight. A number of them always died. They had to be fed and watered, and the only way to do this was to get them off the train, feed and quarter them in large pens with ready handlers and then herd them back on. Then there was the simple math: only 40 percent of a cow's mass is edible. It made no sense to ship the live animal. But to *whom* did it not make sense?

The organizations doing the shipping were mostly cattle brokers. They bought from the stockyards, the vast gathering points for live cattle. They sold to the slaughterhouses that stood in the hundreds, one or two or more at the end of every line. Between were the rail companies, which, though the livestock business was a smelly one and very messy, enjoyed a handsome profit in shipping a high-demand necessity across the country. The business model was working at both ends and in the middle.

It took someone like Gustavus Swift, a slaughterhouse owner at the wrong end of the rail lines, to see the inefficiencies and, just on the other side of these, the possibilities.

He watched the early experiments in rail shipment of dressed meat with interest. These early efforts failed because they packed the meat directly with ice or too close to it, and the color and flavor of the meat was leached out. The experiments were abandoned as a loss and a failure.

Swift had a better idea and drafted a new rail car design. He placed ice bunkers at either end of the rail car with the dressed carcasses on hooks in the center. With the dressed beef hanging from the rafters, however, the cars had a tendency to sway and tip on the curves, and the cars occasionally derailed. In 1868, he sold this design to a Detroit meatpacker, George A. Hammond, who found them better than the alternative. Hammond went on to build a series of cars and used ice harvested from the Great Lakes to cool them.

Swift kept at the problem. In 1877, he hired engineer Andrew Chase to redesign rail cars for his purposes. Chase put the ice bunkers in a shallow, enclosed tray across the top of the car and packed the meat tightly in a well-insulated and well-ventilated compartment at the bottom. The design was the breakthrough the industry needed, both to successfully ship meat and, more importantly, to establish itself as an industry. "Chase's design proved to be a practical solution to providing temperature-controlled carriage of dressed meats, and allowed Swift & Company to ship their products all over the United States, and even internationally, and in doing so radically altered the meat business."[10]

The first refrigerated cars (typically called *reefers*) were 41 feet long and 9¼ feet wide, carrying a thirty-ton payload of which about nine tons was ice. Reefers were wood-framed with tongue-in-groove wood siding. Plywood walls and floors in the interior provided a layer of insulation, and a variety of materials were tried within the walls to further insulate the cargo. Linofelt, an early flax fiber insulation, gave way in the 1920s to a horse-hair product called Hairfelt.[11]

Eventually, refrigerator rail car design returned to Swift's earlier model, with bunkers at each end where ice could be chipped and densely stacked. Ice was loaded through hatches on the top of the cars. Inside the cars, vents between the ice bunkers and meat compartment kept the meat cool, while drains allowed the meltwater to run off. This basic car design survived with only minor alterations until mechanical refrigeration units with onboard engines to run them were introduced starting in the late 1940s.

By the time L.R. Phillips arrived at Swift and Company in 1912, the firm owned a subsidiary called the Swift Refrigerator Line and was operating over three thousand of its own cars. It also owned and operated a string of ice plants along the rail lines to the East Coast.

Young Phillips likely rose to a leadership role in refrigeration during his short time at Swift. Likely, because when he left to serve in the army during World War I five years later, he was made captain, assigned to the Army

Blanche and Leon Phillips, circa 1923. *Connie Phillips collection.*

Construction Corps and given oversight of all refrigeration for all perishable army stores in the United States and France, France being the staging area for U.S. troops and supplies in Europe.

When the war ended, Phillips went to work for the Arctic Ice Machine Company of Canton, Ohio. Arctic developed and sold brine tank ice manufacturing plants using ammonia refrigeration. A year later, Phillips went west. West was a land where the ice business was still expanding rapidly. He took a position as chief engineer with C.M. Gay & Son of Los Angeles. Gay also built brine tank ice plants and installed them at sites across the country.

It was at C.M. Gay & Son that Phillips and Dalzell apparently hooked up.

Whether Phillips knew Dalzell earlier is unclear. Ted Dalzell, grandson of T.P. Dalzell, said the two men met at Cornell, but Cornell has no record of T.P. attending. And they probably did not meet in the military; while Phillips served in the army during World War I, Dalzell was starting and operating three separate car-related companies in Ohio.[12]

Dalzell, born near tiny Dalzell, Ohio, was the same age as Phillips. His mother died when he was young and his father when he was twenty-three. While it is unlikely that Dalzell attended college, and he almost definitely did not graduate, he found success. In Michael James Phillips's (no relation to L.R.) *The History of Santa Barbara County*—a book of descriptions and short biographies for which the subjects generally paid—he describes Dalzell's early development in broad strokes: "T. Paul Dalzell acquired knowledge of the heating and ventilating business early in life. He studied civil and mechanical engineering and for some time was identified with construction work in the Middle West."[13]

This seems largely untrue, and Dalzell himself would at times claim himself as a designer of ice plants, which he clearly was not. Puritan bought its plants, designs and all, from companies like C.M. Gay & Son, and Leon Phillips, with his degree and experience, would have been more likely to design a new plant than Dalzell.

What is known about Dalzell is that by 1917, while World War I raged in Europe, he had launched both the Dalzell Motor Car Company in Youngstown, Ohio, and Liberty Motor Sales in East Liverpool, Ohio. A year later, he incorporated the Youngstown Auto Top Company. With this little empire, he became the dealer for Stutz, Marmon and Chevrolet in the state of Ohio. However, according to a later history of the company, "things were not so good in the automobile business."[14]

Just as unlikely seems the confluence of Dalzell with Constance Lowell. But Dalzell does seem to be the connection. Constance Lowell, born Constance

Percival and Constance Lowell, 1908. *Lowell Observatory Archives.*

Savage Keith in 1863, was a real estate broker in the Boston area who, at forty-four, married the fifty-three-year-old astronomer and millionaire Percival Lowell. Percival built the still-operating Lowell Observatory in Flagstaff, Arizona, and, using its telescope, became famous for his careful observations of the water channels on Mars, from which he deduced that the planet was inhabited. Not only inhabited, in fact, but civilized. Lowell wrote, "The Martian folk are possessed of inventions of which we have never dreamed. With them the electrophone and kinetiscope are things of the bygone past, preserved with veneration in museums as relics of the clumsy contrivances of simple childhood of the race."[15]

Lowell died in 1916, leaving Constance the bulk of his $2 million estate, the remainder to be used to maintain the observatory. Constance fought the will for ten years before the courts decided in favor of the observatory's claim. In the meantime, she'd reduced the Lowell estate by over half.[16]

A large chunk of that reduction, some $250,000, was invested in Puritan Ice.

Based on stories from the late 1930s about Constance Lowell giving Dalzell several old carriages and motorcars for use on his Santa Ynez Valley ranch and for the Fiesta Parades, it does seem to prove that Dalzell was her connection to the Puritan Ice Company investment.

In William Lowell Putnam's *Percival Lowell's Big Red Car*, he states that Puritan Ice was "an investment Mrs. Lowell got into on one of her visits to California."[17] Which leaves the question of how Dalzell ended up in Los Angeles by 1920 working at C.M. Gay & Son as a sales manager.

All that is known now is that T.P. Dalzell's automotive businesses in Ohio were struggling and that he was on the payroll at C.M. Gay & Son, 2,500 miles away, by 1920.

Less than two years after their arrival in Los Angeles, T.P. and L.R. were business partners, living in Santa Barbara and overseeing the building of their first ice plant. However it happened, Phillips and Dalzell, two men with no credentials for going toe-to-toe with the likes of Union Ice or Pacific Fruit Express, left C.M. Gay & Son toward the end of 1921 or in early 1922 and came to Santa Barbara. In their hand they held the proverbial golden ticket: a contract from PFE to supply ice on California's Central Coast, just months before the news would break that lettuce and carrots and other fresh produce would no longer flow south from Salinas to a ready market in Los Angeles.

The Ice Plan

Phillips's and Dalzell's Santa Barbara business plan was initially to fulfill their PFE contract and ice rail cars as they headed south. Salinas Valley lettuce and carrots did not pass through Santa Barbara, but seafood coming from the wharves of San Francisco and citrus shipments originating in Santa Barbara or Goleta required ice.

The partners incorporated Puritan Ice Company on March 2, 1922, and leased an undeveloped space in the midst of the Santa Barbara rail yards where a railroad spur from the main Southern Pacific rail track could easily be built to the proposed icehouse. For the next sixty-plus years, the company's address would be 325 East Cabrillo Boulevard, halfway between the train passenger terminal and the Spanish-style roundhouse where Fess Parker's Doubletree Resort now stands. The site was just north of what had formerly been the Shore Acres Motor Court, an informal, sand-edged parking lot with small palm-thatched huts and beachside palapas that had probably been a little too close to the industrial side of Santa Barbara for tourists.

The plant went in quickly. It was built by the Puritan Ice partners' former company, now called Gay Engineering Corporation. (Norman Gay had renamed the firm in 1922, as his father and founder of C.M. Gay had been deceased for five years, and Norman Gay began a significant reinvention of the company as the premiere ice manufacturing plant designer and builder on the West Coast.)[18]

In a brief *Santa Barbara Morning Press* newspaper article, the completion of the plant in late December was noted.[19] The plant had a fifty-ton-per-day ice manufacturing capacity and a five-hundred-ton storage capacity. It was, like most ice plants of the day, made up of three low, connected, boxy buildings. The heart of the place was the ice plant, where the ice tanks sat and the compressors ran. Next to that, connected by a loading dock, was the storage building.

Pacific Fruit Express built a small office for its lone representative some twenty feet from the icehouse where he could easily observe the icing of the rail cars. Southern Pacific ran a spur line alongside the plant. Out to that line, Puritan built an ice conveyor that trundled the three-hundred-pound blocks of ice from the plant up to a platform that stood two feet above the tops of a line of refrigerator cars. From there, a separate conveyor moved the blocks along the platform.

With the completion of the plant, Puritan was now open for business. It held the contract with PFE for icing all rail-bound perishables in the region

Puritan Ice, Santa Barbara, plant #1, circa 1923. *Connie Phillips collection.*

between the cities of San Luis Obispo, Chatsworth, Montalvo and Saugus, in addition to all perishable freight through Santa Barbara.

Even so, if you were well connected in the local business community and were to stand on the Puritan loading dock as the first block of ice passed to the conveyor, you could be forgiven if you said under your breath to your neighbor, "I don't envy these poor saps. There's simply no demand for fifty tons of ice a day!" This was an experiment doomed to failure or, at best, a slow faltering existence.

The neighbor might nod in knowing agreement. Santa Barbara citrus did not require much ice and only seasonally. Little enough seafood came south—Santa Barbara and San Pedro were working ports. And, at that moment in time, Salinas Valley vegetables still fed Los Angeles and San Diego on rail lines that ran through the Central Valley—the Santa Margarita Agreement was yet to be handed down.

Your neighbor, nodding his head, might turn to you and utter his own news. "Yes, but they've already broken ground for another plant in Guadalupe, just as big."

Guadalupe? Guadalupe had never shipped a box of produce.

Chapter 2

Creating Guadalupe's Salad Days

In 1921, the amount of lettuce grown in the Santa Maria Valley was not tabulated. It was consumed locally. More precisely, it was grown, trucked, sold and consumed in and around the Santa Maria Valley. Some of the lettuce and other field produce was sent "dry-pack" to Santa Barbara and Los Angeles, but the method—trucking produce direct from fields to markets without ice—resulted in high losses, especially during the hotter months of the peak growing season.

In 1922, for the first time, the Santa Maria lettuce crop was measured in rail carloads, with every one of those carloads originating at Puritan Ice Company's Guadalupe plant. Refrigerator cars were rolled to the brand-new 250-foot-long icing platform—the cars and platform were owned by Pacific Fruit Express—next to Puritan Ice Company's brand-new thirty-five-ton ice manufacturing plant. Ice was ferried to the tops of the train cars, broken into chunks and dropped into the ice bunkers at either end of the cars. Then the iced cars were rolled down a separate spur line to the packing sheds. The lettuce was loaded, a paltry total of 168 carloads in 1922, and the cars were assembled onto freight trains running south.

In 1923, 715 carloads of lettuce were shipped, a 325 percent increase. For the first time in the Santa Maria Valley, an iced perishable product could now be shipped to distant cities.

But the produce did not come from nowhere. Neither was it being stacked and consumed in great quantities locally before 1922. Puritan Ice, run by two men who'd never run an ice plant or ice company before, took a page out of Southern Pacific's book and created a complex and large-scale agriculture sideline business that was designed to sustain its core ice business.

THE SOUTHERN PACIFIC ICE PACT

It was not just the slaughterhouses like Swift and Armour—Armour, a Swift competitor, had grown to be the largest refrigerated car operator by the dawn of the twentieth century—that struggled with the best way to ship perishables. As cities grew and factories attracted thousands of people in from the fields, farmers, too, could see their markets, hungry for their products, just across the horizon in towns and cities all across America.

Popularly, the problems for shipping farm produce were believed to be in the same vein as Adam Trask's fictional shipment of six carloads of Salinas Valley lettuce in John Steinbeck's *East of Eden*:

> *As the train came to Sacramento a snow slide closed the Sierras for two days, and the six cars stood on a siding dripping their ice away. On the third day the freight crossed the mountains, and that was the time for unseasonable warm weather throughout the Middle West. In Chicago there developed a confusion of orders—no one's fault—just one of those things that happens, and Adam's six cars of lettuce stood in the yard for five more days. That was enough, and there is no reason to go into it in detail. What arrived in New York was six carloads of horrible slop with a sizable charge just to get rid of it.*[20]

The problems appeared incumbent on the food producers themselves to solve. Their goods were spoiling. Their income—in fact, their business model—was at stake. Like Swift and Armour, it seemed obvious that they should be designing and building refrigerator cars and packaging, working out icing and re-icing programs and paying the railroads extra for expedited shipping. But it was the railroads that increasingly shouldered these burdens because in many cases, and more so in the West, organized groups of food producers—organized enough to fill a rail car—simply did not exist.

Southern Pacific was the railroad of the West more than any other. Southern Pacific experienced the same problems that other rail carriers

Early Pacific Fruit Express refrigerator car, circa 1910. *Pacific Fruit Express archives.*

experienced with perishables but with greater immediacy and with more at stake. Southern Pacific's lines in the early 1900s stretched from Sacramento and Oakland south to Los Angeles and beyond. Another line went east up over the Sierras, ending at Ogden Utah. Here the cars would be transported farther east by other railroad carriers. Other lines snaked from Los Angeles across the southern edge of the country into Texas. The cities and towns it served were few and far between. Heat was a factor for much of the year. Because of the heat and distance, perishable food was local freight at best. It didn't travel well. The company, connecting the dots on the sparsely populated backside of the country, was struggling to fill its trains with passengers and freight.[21]

To overcome these constraints, the Southern Pacific Company sold off selected parcels of land it owned along its routes to establish towns and farms and, in a more wide-ranging and empire-building effort, built the physical, business and marketing infrastructure required to ship and sell perishable goods.

The company's first efforts were focused on singular events such as highly touted and advertised special produce trains from specific geographic areas.

The produce was packed in ventilator ice cars and expedited to larger markets to the south and east. But the distance covered by these trains was relatively short, otherwise spoilage was too high, and getting the interest of sellers and buyers at the two ends of the rail line was difficult. Sellers were often small and separated by both miles and methods. At the other end, the buyers—established brokers and markets and their customers—often unfamiliar with the products being shipped in and not accustomed to the idea of buying something fresh that had traveled hundreds or thousands of miles, were reluctant guinea pigs in the process.

To change minds on both ends meant creating an effective infrastructure in between so that there would be no "carloads of horrible slop" delivered. Instead, there would be crisp green heads of lettuce, crunchy orange carrots and robust tufts of cauliflower and broccoli. And a marketing barrage that would ensure an expectant audience or at least one willing to try the new or off-season items.

Southern Pacific tested the market using refrigerator cars and began acquiring them. By 1900, the company owned nearly one thousand reefer cars. Icing stations were built on runs where there was access to lake or river ice, such as on the track over the Sierra Nevadas. The number of carloads, the lifeblood of the rail business, increased. In 1905, thirty thousand refrigerated rail cars traveled out of California, some 40 percent of these on the then-combined Southern Pacific and Union Pacific lines.

But many of these cars were contracted for use from Armour and other car owners. These car owners were leasing the reefer cars for produce primarily to fill and profit from them on the way back to Chicago. These car owners charged high rates, shuttled cars about to suit their own needs and cared little for the fates of the small produce cooperatives that were organizing themselves to get their products to market. The use of refrigerated cars demanded a more focused and more profitable business model.

In 1906, during the first period when Union Pacific and Southern Pacific were combined (they would merge again in 1996), the conglomerate incorporated Pacific Fruit Express as a subsidiary. Pacific Fruit Express (PFE) was formed to build, lease and operate railroad refrigerator cars and, through Southern Pacific's concentrated campaign, to fill these cars with perishables. Pacific Fruit Express would soon become the largest refrigerator car operator in the world.[22]

Making a large commitment, PFE placed its first order for 6,600 refrigerator cars in December 1906, paying $1,900 apiece. In 1908, it erected a company-owned icing plant in Roseville, California, just outside

Sacramento. This would become the largest ice plant on the planet. In quick succession, other plants would follow.

The concentrated Southern Pacific campaign to move produce from the West to the East was the first of its kind. Across Southern and Central California, Southern Pacific launched experimental farms and contracted with local ice companies to build large rail yard icing plants. If there were regions where produce was not being grown or livestock raised and it appeared that there could be, and the company had rails nearby, Southern Pacific put in test farms and advertised the certain agricultural bounty in the region to attract more farmers. Where farmers sold locally and individually, the railroad helped them organize themselves into cooperatives to increase production, fill long lines of rail cars and market in unison to consumers to the south, north and east to increase the consumption of their produce.

Phillips and Dalzell arrived in Guadalupe in 1922 prepared to do something similar. The year after their ice plant opened in the small farming town, Puritan Ice launched its second company of many to come. It was called California Lettuce Growers, Inc. But California Lettuce may have been an afterthought. California Lettuce was formed in response to what turned out to be a significant failure of Puritan's original business model in the area.

The Lettuce Train

After a brief flurry of shipments and success in the early months of Puritan Ice at Guadalupe came disappointment and failure.

Like most rural ice plants, Puritan Ice Company's manufacturing and storage facilities at Guadalupe were the anchor to a larger, thriving site. Nearby, threaded with rail spurs and roadways to the fields, were the packing sheds. These were typically built by either Southern Pacific or the ice manufacturer and were often sited on land owned or leased by one of those enterprises.

Puritan erected the first nearby packing shed across the road from its new plant in Guadalupe. The company leased it for next to nothing to local farming group Dunbar-Hanson. There were additional discussions and possibly shipments for other local grower-shippers such as Sawdy Hunt, Ward Fruit, American Fruit Growers, Tracey-Waldron, Armbuster and W.M. Watson.[23]

Puritan Ice, Guadalupe plant #2, with three packing sheds, circa 1925. *Rennie Pili collection.*

With a flurry of activity in early July 1923, Dunbar-Hansen harvested lettuce from three hundred acres of Santa Maria Valley farmland, and Puritan iced its first full-scale shipment. But a few short months later, Dunbar-Hansen left the valley, choosing to focus its efforts in the larger and more developed Salinas Valley.

None of the firms Puritan sought early contracts with, including Dunbar-Hansen, were headquartered in the Santa Maria Valley. Based in the quickly growing lettuce empires of the Salinas and Imperial Valleys, these firms chose to maximize their investments in infrastructure in these larger, better-irrigated regions and did not remain in Guadalupe.

Another factor may have been Guadalupe's reputation as a den of iniquity. In a *Santa Barbara Morning Press* newspaper article from 1922, a piece on the small north county town was headlined "Booze, Gambling, Vice Wide Open at 'Little Tijuana' of Santa Barbara County." The article went on to say, "Gin, gambling, girls—all of the facilities for sowing any of the standard varieties of wild oats are present in Guadalupe—provided only that one's tastes are not too fastidious." Migrant farm workers, the article held, fueled the problem, while county officials turned a blind eye or even openly participated.

Whatever the cause for Dunbar-Hansen's retreat from Guadalupe, Puritan Ice had an expensive thirty-five-ton-a-day ice plant that was threatening to go idle before the paint was dry.

A second packing shed had been built by the innocuously named Guadalupe Produce Company next to the Dunbar-Hansen shed. Guadalupe Produce was at least based locally. But the company was operated by Setsuo Artani, who had barely been in town for six months. Puritan doubted this little firm's ability to step up its production to keep a thirty-five-ton-a-day ice plant busy, even during the harvest season.

So Puritan determined to take matters into its own hands. On July 25, 1923, Puritan incorporated California Lettuce Growers, Inc. The directors were scattered through Central California: L.R. Phillips; M.B. O'Brian of El Centro; J.L. Fuller of Heber, California; Frederick Noble of Oxnard; and C.L. Chrisman of Ventura. The firm was capitalized at $100,000, and each share was valued at $100. Each director bought one share.[24]

In the ensuing months, California Lettuce Growers took over the Dunbar-Hansen packing shed, hired Holmes Tabb of Santa Maria to run the company, purchased or leased over one thousand acres of prime farmland in the Guadalupe Valley and planted lettuce, lettuce and more lettuce.[25] It acquired field laborers, tractors, seed and irrigation pipes as needed.

By planting lettuce in such quantities, Puritan was following the successful models of the Salinas and Imperial Valley growers. Puritan saw lettuce as the fastest-growing market, the easiest market to tap into and the most profitable. Now it just had to support the business model with plenty of ice.

Ice Hardware

To support the expected success of the lettuce business in the Santa Maria Valley, Puritan had built the Guadalupe plant as a sister site to the Santa Barbara plant. The two plants were nearly identical in layout. Walter Docker, a former employee at the Santa Barbara plant, detailed the running of the Santa Barbara plant. Rennie Pili, an eventual owner of the Guadalupe plant, provided details of that operation.[26]

The Santa Barbara plant produced fifty tons of ice a day and could store five hundred tons. In Guadalupe, it made thirty-five tons a day and could store five hundred tons. Both plants were designed and built by the entrepreneurs' old employer, Gay Engineering. The plants consisted of an ice-making facility, a loading dock for truck deliveries, an ice storage room and a long, raised

1. Cooling tower
2. Compressor
3. Overhead crane
4. Ice can
5. Ice harvesting
6. Brine tank
7. Ammonia coils
8. Dipping trough

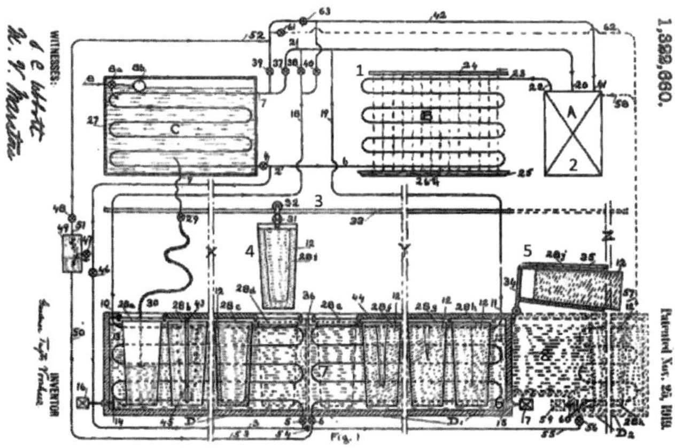

Ice-making apparatus patent plan, similar to that used by Puritan ice plants, 1918. Captions added. Design submitted by George T. Voorhees, owner of Santa Barbara Ice. *United States Patent Office.*

Puritan Ice, Guadalupe plant #2, enlarged icing platform, circa 1928. *Rennie Pili collection.*

icing platform built alongside the adjacent rail spur. Ice was delivered to the platform from the plant by an inclined conveyor.

For the ice-making portion of the facility, Puritan used a closed-cycle ammonia refrigeration system. The cycle began with gasoline- or diesel-powered engines that compressed ammonia gas in a steel chamber. As the gas compressed, it liquefied and its temperature rose precipitously. The gas was then released into a coil of metal tubing that was exposed to air, typically in a cooling tower with water pumped over the coils to speed the cooling. The compressors continued to build pressure on the liquid ammonia in the tubing, and the water continued to battle the rising heat of the ammonia. When the ammonia built up significant pressure in the coils—the target for making ice is around 150 pounds per square inch (psi)—it was released through an expansion valve into the refrigeration unit.[27]

As the ammonia passed through the expansion valve, passing from very high pressure to very low pressure, it expanded to a gas again. The pressure was allowed to drop to between fifteen and thirty psi, depending on the temperature desired. At fifteen psi, the gas temperature dropped to zero degrees Fahrenheit. At thirty psi, it was closer to fifteen degrees. Now, instead of being in tubes exposed to air or water, the ammonia could run through metal piping that passed through a saltwater, or brine, solution. Brine has a lower freezing point than water. The cold temperature of the ammonia gas pulled the heat out of the surrounding brine solution, cooling it to around ten degrees. Water freezes at thirty-two degrees Fahrenheit. When submerged in the brine in ice cans, the water froze.

The ice manufacturing portion of the plants that Gay Engineering built for Puritan were laid out in two side-by-side areas. On one side, on an open concrete pad, the large compressors were bolted to the floor. The other half of the plant contained the brine tank, enclosed behind a low concrete wall approximately four feet high. The tank was piped with galvanized steel tubing and then filled with brine. Into this solution, the ice cans filled with fresh water were lowered with an overhead traveling crane. Once the cans were in place, oak-plank covers were laid over the tops, giving the space an appearance not unlike an empty dance hall. The covers both insulated the ice cans and allowed walking access for the ice crews.[28]

The ice cans would be filled with water—both the Santa Barbara and Guadalupe plants had wells tapped on the premises—and would then be lifted and moved in trays of six cans by the overhead crane to their position in the brine tanks. Lowered into place, the crane was disconnected from the ice cans and the covers dropped back in place.

Twenty-four hours later, the ice was ready. The trays were hoisted out by the crane and trundled to the loading platform where they were dipped in a warm water bath to loosen the blocks from the trays. The trays would then be hooked to a steel frame that allowed the crew to tip the ice blocks, three hundred pounds apiece, out onto the platform. The blocks were then pulled or carted off to the storage buildings. Then the ice trays in the steel frame were righted, and fresh water was poured into them to start the process over again.

During the winter and fall months, when harvests were off and the ice demand low, the three-hundred-pound blocks of ice—roughly four feet tall, two feet wide and one foot deep—were hauled off to storage. The windowless storage buildings were well insulated. They were constructed of two layers of tongue-and-groove one- by four-inch redwood planks. Between these layers was a one-and-three-quarters-inch lining of cork. The exterior walls were tarpapered and plastered.

Workers trundled or dragged the ice blocks to the farthest, darkest corner of the structure and started a layer. In Santa Barbara, the stacking was always on-end, the ice blocks remaining upright as the layers rose through what were eventually three stories of storage. This accommodated the handcarts used to move the ice in and out of storage, and on the elevator they used a wooden platform that lifted one handcart and one ice block to the top level of the ice, wherever that was in the building.

In Guadalupe, also starting in the darkest, deepest corner, the ice was laid flat in a single-story room. Neither facility used sawdust or burlap to insulate the blocks. The ice, once it was in the storage room, created its own environment, cold enough to retard the melting of the ice.

During the spring and summer, much of the newly manufactured ice was sent directly to the platforms to ice the trains, and the winter ice was pulled from storage to make up the shortages.

ICING ON THE TRAIN

Icing of reefers filled with produce took place in Guadalupe. In Santa Barbara, produce cars and cars from farther north carrying meat and seafood were generally re-iced. The capacity of a reefer car was nine thousand pounds of

Icing a rail car, site unknown, circa 1930. *Santa Barbara Public Library.*

ice. Re-icing took less ice than icing an empty car, the quantity depending on weather and the amount of time since the last topping off of the ice.

In Santa Barbara, like at most icing stations, an icing platform fifteen car lengths long and sixteen feet off the ground was erected. At first, just one rail spur paralleled the platform on the north side. The platform stood on pillars and had a wooden walkway about twenty feet wide and a conveyor that ran down the middle. Between six and ten cars were iced at once. But since the icing track was a spur—the first car in was the last car out—a smaller number of cars, maybe five to eight, were accommodated at any one time. As demand increased, a second spur was laid on the opposite side of the platform.

Ice was delivered to the platform from the cold storage building. In Santa Barbara, a "loader" brought the ice down to the loading dock from the elevator on handtrucks. At the loading dock, he would set the blocks on their side and slide them onto a chain-driven conveyor that carried the blocks to the top of the platform. On top, a man snagged each block as it arrived and dragged it onto a conveyor that ran down the center of the platform.[29]

Down the platform, twelve to twenty men hovered over the reefers pulled alongside. The platform did not extend over the reefer cars. Small wooden decks of three to five six-inch planks projected out over the cars. A "pipe man" pulled the ice blocks from the conveyor, laid them on their side and hauled them out onto the wooden deck.

A "bar man" worked the reefers. He opened the reefer hatches and either dropped entire blocks into the ice compartments or, as the compartments filled up, began hacking the ice into smaller chunks that would fill in the crevices, creating a densely packed ice bunker. This hacking took place on the icing platform; hacking the ice while it was in the reefer endangered the ice bunker lining.

Icing a car took two men twenty to thirty minutes for each end, depending on how much ice was needed. In Santa Barbara during the peak growing season, a crew of eight to ten men worked in three 'round-the-clock shifts—7:00 a.m. to 3:00 p.m., 3:00 p.m. to 12:00 a.m. and 12:00 a.m. to 7:00 a.m. A group of ten cars would take a crew of eight about an hour.

The crews iced every car identically, but cars carrying seafood, usually heading south from San Francisco, required salting of the ice to further reduce the temperature. Salt speeds the melting of ice, which decreases the temperature. This was part of Walter Docker's role at Puritan during his years there. He was responsible for delivering different quantities of salt to the icing crews for topping the ice for different types of perishables. Shrimp required an 8 percent solution; fish, 10 percent. The percentages were literal: ten pounds of salt were used for every one hundred pounds of ice. For a nine-thousand-pound load of ice, a 10 percent salt treatment meant nine hundred pounds of salt.

The seafood reefer cars were also slightly different than other reefers. Freight trains ride rough. Their undercarriages were stripped down and less expensive than those for passenger trains. Connecting a freight car to a passenger train passed the rougher ride along, its jars and jerks and shivers transferred to other cars in the train. But passenger trains have always held a higher priority on the rails than freight trains. In order to expedite certain high-cost perishables—especially lobster, shrimp and other seafood—reefer cars were made using the higher-quality carriages. This allowed those cars to be hooked onto a passenger train to ensure a more timely delivery.

For lettuce and carrots and other crated produce, the packing sheds would receive the cars already iced and load them, further icing the lettuce and the crates as they went. The packers worked on long tables, slicing away the outer leaves and otherwise trimming the produce. Then they packed it into lightweight wooden crates, a layer at a time. Ice grinders shredded the blocks of ice from Puritan, and over each layer of produce the workers slid a shovelful of shaved or chipped ice.[30]

When a crate was full, the packers tacked the lids down by hand. The crates were then loaded into the refrigerator cars and "dry-iced" with chunk ice laid down over the top tier of the load.[31]

Puritan used California Lettuce to stoke this ice machinery with as much lettuce as it could grow.

Odd Little Man

Setsuo Aratani, shipping his produce from the second of Puritan's sheds, did not inspire immediate confidence at Puritan. Puritan saw itself in the larger scheme of California produce, and in 1922 and the years immediately after, this meant lettuce.

Aratani did ship lettuce, but it was by no means his sole focus. He kept tinkering. His second year in the sheds, he shipped 34 rail cars of cauliflower and 2 of carrots. By 1926, Aratani was still dutifully shipping lettuce at a rate of 1,774 carloads. But he also shipped 357 cars of cauliflower, 175 of carrots and, another of his experiments that was beginning to work, 204 carloads of mixed vegetables, individual crates inside these cars filled with separate compartments of broccoli, cauliflower, carrots and lettuce.

Aratani already knew the hazards of a single-crop farm and, right with it, the single-crop town. Lettuce was a summer crop. It grew fast. Two plantings a year could be jammed in during the months from June through September. But unless other crops were grown that gave back to the soil what lettuce took out, the soil would soon be depleted and subsequent lettuce crops would become increasingly tasteless and discolored.

A single-season crop also meant single-season income. Even if Aratani could make the lettuce crop pay for the year, it still meant itinerant workers with itinerant values and itinerant earnings to spend in Guadalupe's "Little Tijuana." Aratani had sought a stable home in America since his arrival from Japan, a home that meshed American and Japanese peoples, where Aratani could stay and develop strong ties and effectively wield his benevolent influence.

There was already a thriving Japanese community in Guadalupe. It was what attracted Aratani there in the first place. Japanese immigrants had started coming to Guadalupe around the turn of the century to work in the newly built Union Sugar plant or to sharecrop in the sugar beet fields nearby. The Japanese quickly replaced what few Chinese there were in the fields. The Chinese, their population effectively frozen following the Chinese Exclusion Act of 1882, were not usually responsive to new ventures such as the Union Sugar mill.[32]

The Japanese filtered into many of the same roles that had been available to the Chinese in California society, but more than any other immigrants, the Japanese took up farming. Designated as aliens by law, their activities were rigidly restricted. Farming was one of the few pursuits a Japanese national could operate on his own, and he could even, if the title was held by a second-generation Japanese American, possess land or businesses. Guadalupe became the center of a thriving hub of small Japanese farms. By 1922, the Guadalupe Japanese Association, supporting Japanese farm operations, had branches in Santa Maria, Oceano, Pismo Beach and San Luis Obispo. The "Japantown" of Guadalupe became an important Japanese commercial center. The Aratanis—leaders in business, church matters and social and sporting events—emerged as the most successful Japanese family in town.

Setsuo Aratani (1885–1940) arrived in the United States from Japan in 1905. He landed in San Francisco, where he studied English and played pick-up baseball in the Japanese community. When the San Francisco Earthquake and the subsequent fires destroyed the better part of that city in April 1906, immigrants living in the city often took the blame for the looting and violence that followed. Aratani found the business climate increasingly difficult and moved to the Los Angeles basin.[33]

In Los Angeles, Aratani took employment as a farm worker in El Monte. After a few years, he leased a small plot and worked his own strawberry farm in the town of Moneta (long since encompassed by Gardena, California, itself a borderless suburb of Los Angeles). While Aratani was farming there, the Alien Land Act of 1913 was passed restricting leases to three years for anyone barred from citizenship. The only peoples barred from citizenship at the time were Asians. Aratani, with no other real options, stuck it out, increasing the size of his leasehold to nine acres in 1914.

Aratani repeatedly was offered and took leadership roles. In 1915, newly married, he was elected president of the Japanese Association of

Guadalupe Produce packing label, circa 1935. Setsuo Aratani played on and was a proponent of the local Japanese baseball teams. *John Perry collection.*

America. He organized and helped cooperatively market the produce of the Japanese growers in the regions where he farmed. In 1915, the Governor of Hiroshima, Aratani's home prefecture, publically recognized Aratani for his achievements. Later, Japan's Prince Fushimi would present Aratani a national award for his leadership of the expatriate Japanese community in America.

In 1920, a second Alien Land Act was passed in California, this time closing many of the loopholes of the first. Asian nationals were now restricted even from leasing farmlands. By now, Aratani was farming in Pacoima in the San Fernando Valley, and though Pacoima won the first prize for farm products at the Los Angeles County Fair in 1921, his eyes were set out of the dusty valley to the tiny farming haven for Japanese: Guadalupe.

The Japanese refuge in Guadalupe was created in large part by the local landowners, who readily created flexible land-use agreements to allow the productive and grateful Japanese to farm sugar beets on their land.

The charismatic and patient Setsuo Aratani arrived in 1921 and worked the fields while he organized a business that would stand legally against the Alien Land Acts. To do this, the company had to be owned by American-born individuals. Aratani created Central Produce Company under the ownership of American-born sons of family friends, Butch

Tamura and Miyochiki Matsumo. In 1922, Aratani signed a lease for six hundred acres and began farming on a large scale.

Ice Needs Produce Needs Ice Needs Produce

Setsuo Aratani must have had Puritan Ice in his sights when he leased his six hundred acres of land. There was no market for six hundred acres worth of produce that did not require ice to get it there. Aratani, the first Japanese grower in the area to do so, approached Puritan and asked it for shed space on its leasehold. Puritan leased him the space.

In order to ramp up his production quickly to meet Puritan's demand, Aratani formed a marketing firm called Guadalupe Produce with two other local Japanese farmers, Naoichi Ikeda and Reiji "Ben" Kodama.[34]

Aratani's courage at approaching the ice company for packing sheds and a toehold in the eastern vegetable market inspired others. H.Y. Minami soon had a packing shed near Puritan. Then in quick succession, C.M. Otoi, Santa Maria Produce, Union Produce and Tomooka Farms, all Japanese growers, were on the Puritan packing site.

Puritan Ice, Guadalupe plant #2, with the Guadalupe Produce and CLG (California Lettuce Growers) sheds in the foreground, circa 1935. *Rennie Pili collection.*

Between Guadalupe Produce and California Lettuce Growers, Puritan iced 715 carloads of lettuce in 1923. This put the Guadalupe ice plant at 30 percent capacity. As the other Japanese farms came up to speed, and as Guadalupe Produce and California Lettuce expanded their capacities, Puritan's ice shipments grew quickly. In 1924, more than 1,000 carloads of lettuce were shipped.

By 1925, Puritan was running at 60 percent capacity, and with acreage and shipments steadily increasing, the growth curve was climbing through the proverbial roof. Phillips and Dalzell brought Gay Engineering back to town and increased the size of the Guadalupe plant.

The Ice Expansion

In 1927, the *Santa Barbara Morning Press* finally got wind of the ice industry in the county and published an in-depth story on Puritan. The article put the amount of ice used by Pacific Fruit Express in the combined San Luis Obispo, Santa Barbara and Ventura Counties at 1,700 tons in 1922. In 1926, 45,000 tons were used. The projection for 1927 was 60,000 tons.[35]

All of this was Puritan Ice production.

"Before the Puritan Ice Company built in Santa Barbara in 1922, there never had been a carload of perishable produce shipped out of here to eastern markets. The year 1927 will see at least 7,000 cars of vegetables shipped to eastern markets from Santa Barbara County."[36] California Lettuce Growers, identified as a subsidiary of Puritan, was listed as shipping 1,000 cars annually and had, in addition to its one thousand acres of Guadalupe farmland, an additional five hundred acres in the Imperial Valley where it grew winter lettuce.

Because of the increase in demand Puritan was facing—and was in fact helping to create—it had embarked on a sizable increase in capacity at its two existing plants.

In 1925, the Guadalupe plant was increased from thirty-five tons of manufacturing capacity a day to one hundred tons and from five hundred tons of storage capacity to one thousand tons. With this expansion came a concentrated streamlining effort for the back end of the ice-making process.

Puritan Ice, Guadalupe plant #2 expansion during 1926–27. *Rennie Pili collection.*

As before, six full ice cans were hoisted in a tray from the brine and delivered to the warm water trough by crane. However, now the ice cans were set onto a hinged steel shelf. The shelf flipped over automatically, and the six ice blocks slid from the cans directly onto a conveyor that ran the breadth of the two side-by-side manufacturing floors. The conveyor then dropped through a slot in the wall and traveled through the plant's three ice storage rooms on successive belts at an ascending angle. The angle allowed crews to pull the ice off at any height in the storage rooms, depending on how high the ice was stacked in that room.

The conveyor then led to a door in the tallest storage structure where, if the ice was still on the conveyor, the ice exited the building, traveled above the rail spur below and was carried out to a new 485-foot icing platform. Thus, the same conveyor system that delivered the ice to the storage buildings was used to send ice to the platforms.

The new process saved a lot of time and muscle.

The Santa Barbara facility also got an overhaul. The 50-ton capacity plant was expanded to 130 tons. Storage of 500 tons was expanded to 3,000 tons. But there was more than one reason for the Santa Barbara plant expansion. Puritan had taken its ice empire to the streets of Santa Barbara, and it was determined to win the domestic ice wars.

Chapter 3

Ice Wars on State Street

Puritan Ice's arrival in Santa Barbara County was unchallenged for the icing of trains. But Puritan quickly invested in a small fleet of REO Speedwagons to deliver ice to homes, butcher stores, groceries, restaurants and bars. On the streets of Santa Barbara, it faced stiff competition.

Santa Barbara had no ice to speak of until the mid-1880s. According to Santa Barbara historical columnist Stella Haverland Rouse, writing in 1965, Santa Barbara received its first deliveries of ice from Union Ice Company's Los Angeles outlets in 1885 or 1886. The ice was harvested from the Truckee River some five hundred miles to the north and probably delivered by steamship, since the first train from Los Angeles did not arrive in Santa Barbara until 1887 (the first train through to San Francisco was not until 1901).

Ice may have been a novelty in the 1880s, but the demand was immediate and real.

A Santa Barbara resident wrote to the editor of the *Santa Barbara Morning Press* in July 1886, "If properly managed, [ice production] would be a paying concern, and the demand would increase with the growth of the town. There is a good ice plant at San Luis Obispo, which is neither larger nor richer than Santa Barbara."[37]

Three short months later, an unnamed company took the letter writer up on the idea. In October 1886, the *Morning Press* announced that a company had been organized "to manufacture ice upon the most approved method and supply it to families at a price which will put it within the reach of all."[38]

Donner Ice cold storage shed, along Truckee River, circa 1890. *Sierra Magazine. Drawing by R.J. Church.*

Aerial of Santa Barbara over lower State Street. Santa Barbara Ice is the low white tower in the lower middle right. Circa 1930. *John Fritsche collection.*

Whether this company ever froze a block of ice is not known. But in the early 1890s, butchers in Santa Barbara were installing cooling rooms and refrigerators, which did not make ice but used delivered ice to cool an insulated space. In 1891, the I.K. Fisher Company "installed a Gurney Dry Air Cooling Room at 711 State for The California Market, and the Santa Barbara Slaughtering Company." The room had six-inch-thick walls lined with asbestos, and the upper portion of the interior room could contain five tons of ice. Meat stored in the lower compartment would keep for up to thirty days.[39]

The purveyor was most likely Union Ice, which maintained an office and cold storage in Santa Barbara. But its hold in town was tentative. In 1895, George E. Voorhees arrived and took control of the town's ice market.

Voorhees was a transplant from Morristown, New Jersey, coming to the West Coast in early 1894 to take on half ownership and management of the new Santa Ana, California ice plant. The City of Santa Ana, calculating the cost of obtaining ice from Union Ice in Los Angeles, decided the town would do better if it helped fund and operate its own plant. Voorhees wrote from Morristown, offering his funds and expertise in exchange for partial ownership, and Santa Ana's town fathers accepted his offer.[40]

In Morristown, Voorhees had been a trustee with his church, the First Presbyterian of Morristown,[41] and acted as a member of the volunteer firemen's group, The Independent Hose Association.[42] What he did there for a living was not recorded, but he came to Southern California with a larger plan than running a five-ton-per-day ice plant in Santa Ana. Santa Barbara became an early, and subsequently his primary, base of operations. Voorhees arrived at the San Marcos Hotel in Santa Barbara on February 5, 1895.[43]

Union Ice was still in town, but Voorhees was not daunted by its presence. He launched a company named Santa Barbara Ice Company and built a modern ice plant at 220 State Street. He did not concern himself with rail icing. With an initial capacity of five tons daily, his wagons trundled through the streets delivering to homes and businesses.

But Voorhees was well aware of the rail business for ice. In 1899, Voorhees traveled to San Bernardino, where the *San Bernardino Sun* reported that "Mr. Voorhees of Santa Barbara made his first visit to San Bernardino, looking for a site for an ice plant." Voorhees interviewed Santa Fe officials "in regard to supplying the road with the ice necessary for its business, and locating the coming plant near the Santa Fe yards." Voorhees set about construction of a 120- by 48-foot brick building housing an ice plant with a capacity of seventeen tons. "This will enable the new plant to compete successfully with the Union Ice Company."[44]

A few weeks later, the *San Bernardino Times-Index* reported, "When it first became known that Mr. Voorhees intended putting in a plant for the manufacture of ice the general opinion was that he would never carry out his intention, for the reason that it was thought that the Union Ice Company would buy him off; in fact it is reported that such an offer was made, but without effect." Planning to produce both domestic ice and rail car ice, "Mr. Voorhees has a contract with the railroad people to supply what ice they can use at this point."[45]

By 1904, Voorhees and Santa Barbara Ice had locked up the local business in Santa Barbara. In a surprising move, the mighty Union Ice of Los Angeles closed its Santa Barbara office as Voorhees cornered local expertise, competitive pricing and a reputation for service. He had come up against Union Ice three times and had held his ground or won each time. If Santa Barbara had an iceman in 1920, it was George E. Voorhees.

ICING THE COMPETITION

In 1920, Voorhees faced a new Santa Barbara competitor. Emmett Ord built an ice plant, Ord Ice Company, at 209 West Canon Perdido Street. Located far from the rail yards, Ord's obvious objective was to chip off a piece of Voorhees's domestic ice market. Possibly in response, Voorhees diversified. That same year, Voorhees opened Flavo Flour Company at his 220 State Street location and began milling flour for delivery to homes and businesses in Santa Barbara.

In 1922, when Phillips and Dalzell came to town, G.E. Voorhees had been in the ice business in Santa Barbara for twenty-seven years.

Unlike Ord Ice, Puritan may not have looked like a threat to Voorhees's core business when it arrived. Its business was centered on the Southern Pacific rail lines and serviced the nonexistent agricultural region to the north. But two years later, Puritan had entered the domestic market aggressively. Between Ord and Puritan, the Santa Barbara Ice Company's local ice delivery business took a significant hit. A price war was underway,

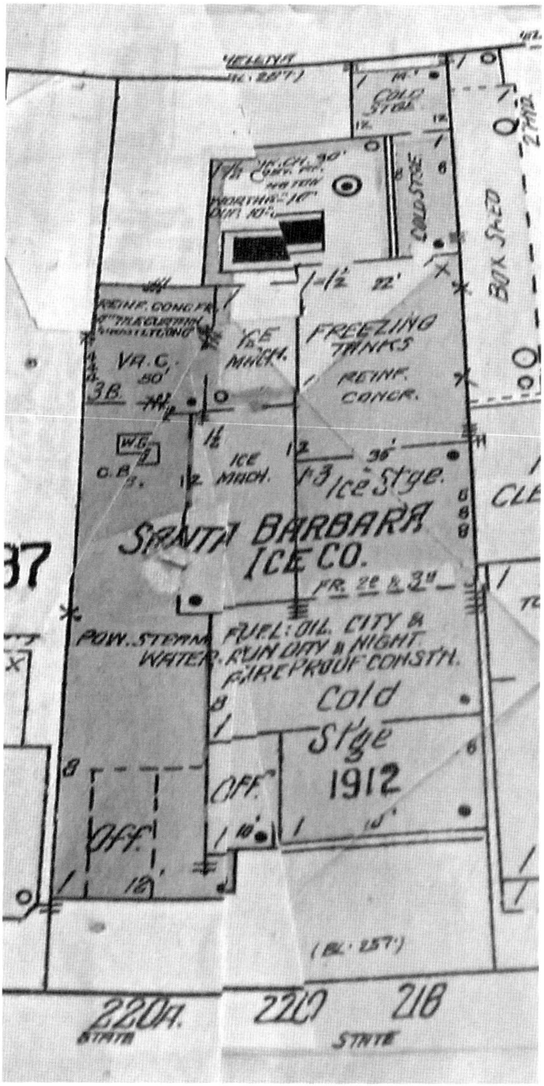

Sanborn Fire Insurance Map showing Santa Barbara Ice in 1930. State Street runs along the bottom of the image. *University of California Santa Barbara, Special Collections.*

and Puritan was winning. As a result of the lower receipts, G.E. Voorhees moved his family first from Montecito to lower San Andres Street and, the year after that, to Haley Street.

In 1924, after two years of battling Puritan and Ord in the streets, Voorhees changed the name of Flavo Flour to Santa Barbara Flour, and he brought in Mathew Roeser to manage it. Then Voorhees hired Santa Barbara attorney Harry W.T. Ross to sue Puritan Ice.

Filed in December 1924, the Voorhees suit stated that Santa Barbara Ice Company had a long-established price of $8.00 per ton for its ice. But Puritan was selling ice in Santa Barbara at $5.00 per ton. It was able to do this because it was selling ice for $10.00 per ton in Guadalupe. Similar prices were in effect for smaller deliveries to homes and businesses. To all appearances "[Puritan] depends on the profits of the Guadalupe branch to maintain its business."[46] The $114,000 unfair business practices suit claimed that Santa Barbara Ice had lost $38,000 in actual damages.

DOMESTIC ICE

Puritan's Guadalupe plant made just one kind of ice. It was called white ice because the ice was a cloudy, opaque white and was used solely for icing vegetables. If you wanted to sell to the domestic market, white ice didn't cut it.

Consumers were originally introduced to ice as a product cut from lakes and rivers. This ice arrived in crystalline blocks you could see through. Competitors, who could not find a free acre of ice in the mountains or a rail contract to haul it back to town, saw a crack in the natural ice companies' business plan. An ice manufacturing plant could churn out ice right in town and avoid the costs of cutting, hauling and melting and some of the storage problems.

As such ice manufacturers began to open, the natural ice companies touted the purity of their freshwater, natural ice over artificial ice: "The testimony of medical men, and all others who have made the subject of pure ice a study, is that natural ice is far preferable to that manufactured in machines. There are on this coast thirteen machines, capable of making from five to fifteen tons daily, but all are idle. They could not compete with the natural production."[47]

The Santa Barbara firm that appeared and disappeared in 1886 exemplified the response. "The originators of this company claim that artificial ice is the only pure article obtainable, and is much healthier than river or lake ice which contains many impurities."[48]

But the consumers decided the matter, at least in the short term. For all the claims that manufactured ice lacked impurities and regardless of the fact

Puritan Ice, Santa Barbara plant #1, circa 1930. The icing platform is barely visible through the trees to the right. *Connie Phillips collection.*

that it was usually less expensive, it was, unlike the clear ice cut from lakes and rivers, a cloudy, opaque white. The white was mostly tiny air bubbles trapped in the quickly cooled water. Nevertheless, it was not something you could chip off and drop in your mother-in-law's glass of iced tea.

In response, ice manufacturers figured out how to create clear ice in the plant. One of the earliest patents to accomplish this was developed by Cassius M. Gay, father of Norman Gay, the family whose firm built the Puritan plants.[49] The concept was a simple one and mimicked, to an extent, the formation of natural ice: agitate the water slightly as it froze. This process forced the tiny, trapped air bubbles in the water to merge and eventually rise and escape.

The method Gay settled on, and the one still in use in large ice manufacturers today, is that of forcing a low flow of compressed air into the ice for half the freezing time. Small, flexible tubes were inserted into the ice cans and hooked to a compressed air system. The larger bubbles and slight agitation in the cooling water shook the smaller bubbles out. Before the ice froze solid, and when the tiny air bubbles were out, the tubes were removed. The result was a three-hundred-pound block of ice you could see through.

There was a cost, however. Clear ice took twice as long to make as white ice. A plant making white ice had double the capacity of an identically sized plant making clear ice. Accordingly, prices were higher for clear ice.

Puritan's Santa Barbara plant made both clear and white ice. To deliver its clear ice, the three-hundred-pound blocks were pulled from cold storage, taken by an ice elevator down to the loading platform and scored using a saw that cut two-inch-deep lines in the blocks. The scoring allowed the men making the home and restaurant deliveries of clear ice to easily break the ice to the weight requested by the ice sign left on the icebox by the resident or restaurant manager.

To service the Guadalupe domestic ice market, clear ice was delivered by train from the Santa Barbara plant. Otherwise, Puritan's REO Speedwagons delivered ice from Goleta down to Ventura.[50] At Ventura, Puritan came up against the invisible but real barrier of Union Ice, well situated in Santa Paula.

DEPRESSION-ERA ICE

The Union line in Santa Paula and Ventura never went away. In fact, Phillips and Dalzell would cede the line in a story that comes in another chapter of the firm's history.

Back in Santa Barbara, the 1924 court case that G.E. Voorhees and Santa Barbara Ice brought against Puritan was settled out of court.[51] What little reached the media about the Santa Barbara Ice lawsuit appeared in the *Santa Barbara News-Press* in June 1925.[52] At a guess, Puritan paid Santa Barbara Ice some amount and reset its prices in the area somewhat higher.

But the damage was already done. Most customers who switched to Puritan did not switch back. Domestic ice pricing may have equalized somewhat, but Puritan was not likely to set its prices higher than Santa Barbara Ice. Puritan, after all, had lucrative contracts with Pacific Fruit Express to keep its coffers full.

The war was over, but it took Voorhees awhile to admit defeat.

In 1931, as the Great Depression settled in and began picking off businesses, Santa Barbara Ice was a casualty. That year Voorhees sold his ice plant, lock, stock and barrel, to L.R. Phillips and T.P. Dalzell of Puritan Ice Company. The company shipped Santa Barbara Ice Company equipment to its recently developed Lompoc facility.

But the competition in Santa Barbara was not completely squashed. Ord Ice remained, but Puritan would resolve this. It was the small splinters and

Roeser & Sons telephone directory advertisement, 1935. *Santa Barbara Public Library.*

shards of domestic ice manufacturing that would continue to nag at Puritan for many years.

In 1932, a small ice distribution facility called City Ice Service was built at 534 East Haley Street in Santa Barbara. Lester Quensel, a former manager for Puritan Ice and, before that, of Santa Barbara Ice, was the owner. Ice was manufactured on the site with a small plant. Evidence of this is the fact that the address supported a string of ice companies for the next decade, the equipment changing hands with each successive owner. (The building today still looks like a utilitarian, low-slung ice plant.)

Quensel barely hung on a year, but the site would remain a thorn in Puritan's side for the rest of the decade. Theodore Ditgen bought the company and ran it for three years. In 1936, Delbert Grunstead and E.A. King were operating ice delivery services from the address. In 1938, W.A. Pace had taken over. It finally faded as an ice company in the mid-1940s. The pressure from the larger and more efficient Puritan was simply too much.

Across town, Mathew Roeser who had been managing Voorhees's Santa Barbara Flour Company for six years, had seen Puritan's invasive business practices firsthand. When Voorhees sold his ice company to Puritan, Roeser moved Santa Barbara Flour Company from 220 State to a site next door at 116 Santa Barbara Street and renamed it Roeser and Sons. In 1934, perhaps seeing light at the end of the Great Depression tunnel, Roeser added an ice plant and began delivering ice. It was the beginning of a tenacious competitor to Puritan for home and business delivery in Santa Barbara. Over the years, the business would change names and move locations, but it would continue to pester Phillips and Dalzell until well into the 1950s.

Two years after opening his ice plant, Roeser sold it to Walter Klehn. Klehn renamed the business Polar Ice and remained at the same location, operating side-by-side with Roeser and Sons as it milled flour and feed. Klehn disappeared not long after, both from Polar and Santa Barbara, and no manager or owner was listed with Polar for the next decade. Roeser may have taken the helm again.

By 1927, both L.R. Phillips and T.P. Dalzell were building new homes on the Riviera in Santa Barbara. This is the Phillips home on Mira Vista, 1927. *Connie Phillips collection.*

In 1939, Puritan and Polar crossed paths more directly. The series of events began when Hubert D. Knickerbocker and Roy V. Horton, both employees of Puritan since 1931, launched Knickerbocker & Horton, manufacturers and dealers in ice. They built a sizable new plant at 205 West Montecito Street and braced for Puritan's wrath.

Whatever the wrath was, it was fast, quiet and effective. The two men sold their company to Polar Ice less than a year after opening, and Knickerbocker and Horton, formerly engineers with Puritan, were now listed as delivery drivers for Puritan, a significant step down the ice ladder. Horton lasted less than a year before he left town. Knickerbocker stayed behind the wheel of an ice truck for two years before he left the business. It would be five years before he would get steady work again, this time for Farallone Fisheries in Ventura as a refrigeration engineer.

Polar, happy with the new ice plant that Knickerbocker and Horton had installed at 205 West Montecito, moved its operations there.

J.E. Rogers was brought in as manager in 1945. A year later, L.B. Clift, Henry Ricks and Andrew and Marvin Berry bought the company and added frozen fruits and vegetables to its offerings. (Frozen foods had been introduced to the mass market by Birds Eye brand in 1930.) In 1947, W.H. Moseley purchased the company. Moseley owned it until it closed, victim of home and restaurant icemakers and refrigerators, in 1959. The site continued to service businesses that required insulated, cooled storage space. The first to take over was M&F Wholesale Meat Packing. Later, Jordano's Wholesale Grocery used the site for many years. The facility is currently operated by fruit and vegetable purveyor The Berry Man.

Through all of these events in Santa Barbara, Puritan, with its anchor site in the rail yards and its money stream from the north, prevailed. Puritan's trucks continued to be the most familiar domestic delivery vans, a fleet of fifteen to twenty trucks running from Ventura to Guadalupe on a daily basis.

But there was another thorn in its side, one that threatened Puritan in Santa Barbara and drew it in the direct line of Union Ice's fire in Oxnard.

Chapter 4

Borders of Empire in Oxnard

In 1920, two years before the arrival of Phillips and Dalzell and Puritan Ice in Santa Barbara, another ice plant opened in Santa Barbara. Located at 209 West Canon Perdido, it was called Ord Ice and was named after local businessman Emmett G. Ord.

Emmett Ord, born in Colusa County, California, on April 1, 1865, and raised in Santa Barbara, was an achiever of sorts. "The career of this well known business man and popular citizen of Santa Barbara seems to indicate that he has not failed to imbibe a due quota of the progressive spirit of the West or to be animated with that self-reliance and resourcefulness that has been characteristic of the people of his native state from the early pioneer epoch to the present time."[53]

He started out in the plumbing and tinning business and then opened a hardware store. He moved his enterprise around, though, landing "at Santa Paula for three years; at Santa Cruz for two years; at Randsburg [California] for 1½ years; and at Bisbec (sp), Arizona, for four years." But after his Randsburg store burned to the ground, and before he moved to Bisbee, he took a jaunt to Mexico City, where he ran a large tin stamping mill.

From Bisbee, he went to Douglas, Arizona, where he erected and ran the first hotel in town. Then he went to Naco, Arizona, where he ran the town's water works. When he finally returned to Santa Barbara, he "engaged in the automobile business, with a substantial and constantly increasing patronage of appreciative order."[54]

Changing his career yet again, at the age of fifty-five, he took a running start at the ice business and, soon after he opened, looked like the man to beat.

Grainy image of the Ord Ice plant at 209 East Canon Perdido. Morning Press, *August 14, 1929.*

The Ord plant was a clear ice plant, more centrally located in town than Santa Barbara Ice. Ord bought a small fleet of trucks and painted each with his logo and motto: *Ord—It's Scored!—Ice.* At the time, Santa Barbara Ice, not having faced serious competition for some time, did not have a scoring machine. Santa Barbara Ice deliverymen eyeballed the ice before cracking off a chunk with a pick or hatchet. The result was customers who also eyeballed the ice and who saw the times when the rough guesstimate of the ice man seemed to be in favor of the ice company or the next customer on the route. Ord offered precision and fairness, and his ice was as good as the competition's.

Ord's trucks were new. His plant was new. His ice was scored. He was direct competition for Santa Barbara Ice and George Voorhees.

Puritan arrived in Santa Barbara two years after Ord opened, and Puritan, too, bought a small fleet of delivery trucks and sent them scurrying up and down the streets. Its motto graced its trucks: "Puritan Ice! Be Perspicacious!"

But just like Santa Barbara Ice, Ord suffered from Puritan's lower prices. Puritan was not just looking to clear the field of Santa Barbara Ice but also the better-capitalized and more modern Ord.

Ord, perhaps watching the machinations and greater security of Puritan, decided that he, too, would venture into the rail ice business. But the Santa Barbara and Santa Maria Valley ice markets were already iced by Puritan.

Southern Lettuce

Where food was concerned, the times were changing. As cities grew and fewer people grew their own food, the newspapers kept a running banter about what was growing where in California and often supplied great detail about the operations. At the dawn of the 1920s, Ventura and Oxnard were largely bean districts when it came to row crops. Green beans and lima beans were hardy and could be transported farther than most other crops without cooling.

In 1923, with the loss of Salinas Valley produce in Southern California due to the Santa Margarita agreement, a shift came. The *Los Angeles Times*, in its weekly collection of farm news from across the southland, reported from Oxnard, "Bean growers of this district are being urged to plant lettuce. Local distributors point out that the seed can be planted in December and the crop harvested in April, the land being cleared in time for planting the bean crop. Lettuce has been found a good rotation crop for bean land. Local growers have planted some acreage already this season and many are favorably inclined toward increasing the acreage."[55]

In a local farmers' meeting at the end of the year, "Lettuce received the main attention of the growers, but cauliflower, spinach, tomatoes, bell peppers and cabbage were all discussed."[56] The Walter Rowe Ranch of Oxnard was experimenting with strawberries with good success. By 1924, "Vegetable growing, practically unknown on a commercial scale here a decade ago, has made great advances. About 1,500 acres have been planted in the past twelve months in the Mound, Oxnard, Camarillo and Saticoy sections. Lettuce, cauliflower, peppers, peas, tomatoes and other garden truck are raised."[57]

It was lettuce that demanded ice. And with the rail icing contracts for Santa Barbara and Guadalupe and points north through San Luis Obispo locked up by Puritan, Ord went south.

Ord started to deliver domestic ice in Oxnard as early as July 1923.[58] He started his search for property immediately after this, letting it be known that he would be building a rail ice plant in the area. In September 1923, just as the growers were getting wind of the changes in the market, Emmett Ord purchased ten commercial lots on the south side of Enterprise Street in Oxnard in order to build his plant.[59]

Ord had taken an option on property owned by W.H. Lathrop earlier in his search for land, but the Lathrop parcel had a private rail crossing on the access road to the property. "A private crossing," Ord explained, "can be blocked at any time, and while an ice truck was waiting for a long freight train to switch cars and pass on, the ice would be melting." The lots Ord eventually purchased, a few hundred feet away from the Lathrop parcel, had a public crossing. No train would block it for long.[60]

On the day of the groundbreaking for the new plant, October 1, 1923, Ord told the small gathering, "People don't realize what's ahead for Oxnard. Oxnard will be three times as large as any other city in the county."[61] He told reporters that he wanted to erect a sign, "some 20 feet high on the side of his buildings near the depot which would read something like 'Oxnard, the home of Ord Ice Compny.'"[62]

During construction, Emmett Ord traveled between Santa Barbara and Oxnard in a state of grace. The Oxnard paper noted his arrivals along with other notables. About to turn fifty-nine, maybe his luck had finally changed, and he had found a niche where he could prosper.

The plant was operational by January 5, 1924. "Brine was turned into the big tank and the 308 cans filled with water. As it takes longer to freeze the first tank of ice, the company will not start 'pulling' the cans until about Tuesday or Wednesday."[63] A 308-can facility would produce approximately forty-five tons of rail (or white) ice daily.

At some point—sometime between 1922 and 1924—Ord had also purchased a site and built a plant in Ventura, probably a small one for domestic delivery purposes only. The local media was quiet about the arrival, but it demonstrated that Ord was building a small empire of ice production on the Central Coast.

But Ord's empire collapsed quickly.

Less than a month after Ord Ice opened in Oxnard, officials from Union Ice appeared in town, kicking stones in vacant lots along the railroad tracks and pointing down the parallel steel rails into the distance.

Ord, already tapped out financially from his Oxnard construction project, immediately announced plans to build a second, larger plant in Oxnard. To finance the venture, he recapitalized Ord Ice Company, offering $100,000 in stock on top of a stock issue of $175,000 from 1922.

On May 3, 1924, Ord had another piece of bad luck. A worker died at his Santa Barbara ice plant. The official cause of death for Peter Bonetti, thirty-five, was a heart attack. But the evidence seemed to point toward electrocution from Ord equipment. "Suddenly, electric current failed and several motors in the building were burned out," the newspaper reported. "The body was found at 5 a.m. Thursday morning on the second deck with no one else around. The lever of the traveling electric crane was still

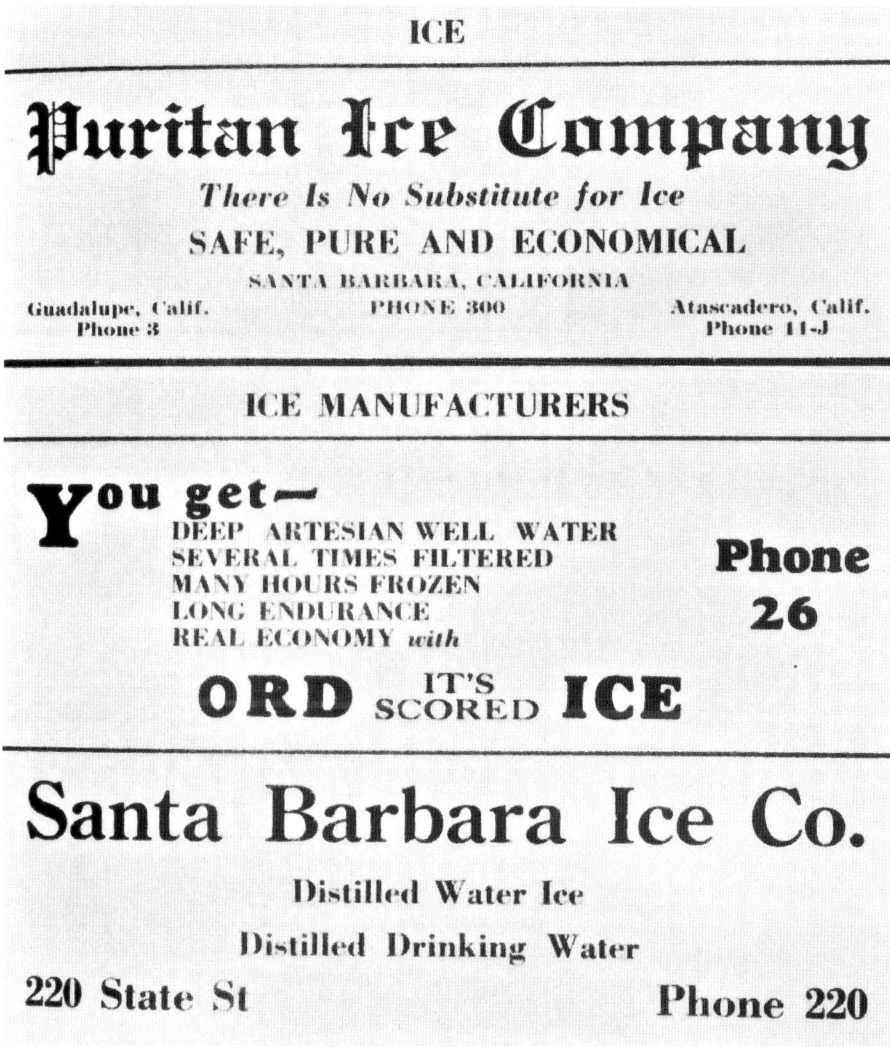

A telephone directory "Buying Guide" during the period when Santa Barbara Ice, Ord Ice and Puritan Ice were competing in 1925. *Santa Barbara Public Library.*

in the dead man's clutch." The paper reported, "All indications pointed to electrocution." But, as there were "no marks on his body," the coroner recorded that Bonetti had suffered a heart attack.[64]

Then, on May 7, Ord traveled to Oxnard on a public relations campaign. On May 9, the front page of the *Oxnard Daily Courier* announced, "Union Ice Buys Site for Ice Plant Near Railroad."[65] Near railroad, in this case, meant just down the tracks from Ord Ice. Ord made sure his expansion plans were part of the story. His strategy was, "We were here first!"

But Union Ice had a reputation for winning its battles, sometimes in ugly ways.

Union Ice has cropped up a few times in this tale already. Now, through Ord, the fate of Union Ice would touch the fate of Puritan Ice. It is unclear what dealings between the firms took place, but as it played out, Ord was sacrificed, and Puritan was left to its rich vein of icing perishable goods from the central California coast.

Union Ice Never Plays Nice

Union Ice came together from six ice firms all plying the San Francisco ice trade in the late 1870s and early 1880s. Competition among the six firms had driven prices down, deliverymen underbid one another at back doors, and the money was simply too thin for the tastes of Lloyd Tevis, a man with ownership in two of the firms. Complaining to a journalist later on, Tevis said, "The retail price of ice was reduced to a half cent a pound and frequently it was given away."[66]

To Tevis, the solution was to merge and monopolize.

The merger of the six ice firms was completed, and the new company, Union Ice, incorporated on November 1, 1882.[67] The company retained the California and Nevada Ice Company headquarters at 735 and 737 Fourth Street in San Francisco, where it ran a cold storage and ice distribution center.

Lawsuits to stop the merger arose immediately. In one suit, John H. Miller of the newly formed Crystal Ice Company, a company expressly incorporated to counter the Union monopoly, was able to get an injunction against his business partner, Windsor A. Keefer. Keefer had taken a bribe from Union and delivered all the ice from the new Crystal Ice plant to

Union's loading docks, essentially reinforcing the monopoly. The media reported on the case, "Prior to the formation of Union there were six independent companies in the field selling ice, and there was great competition in the business, but those six companies decided to pool their issues and establish an exclusive monopoly."[68]

By December 1882, Union Ice was sending Jacob Hoehm to locate a site for a storage and distribution facility in Los Angeles. Hoehm, who would serve as general superintendent in Los Angeles, purchased a double lot at the corner of First and Alameda, the address numbers 15 and 17 Alameda Street. The company began at once to build "a handsome storehouse at the same location." "This ice," Hoehm assured the press, "is frozen on the waters of the Truckee River, which receives its supply from Lake Tahoe and is given by scientists to be the best water ever known."[69]

In the next few years, Union would spread quickly to Fresno, Colton, Riverside, Ventura, Redlands, Pomona, Bakersfield, Pasadena and, of course, Santa Barbara. Still tied closely to river and lake ice, the locations it built were cold storage facilities with a fleet of horses and wagons. Ice was moved by rail from Union's sources in the Sierras and between the various distribution sites.

In these towns, if there were ice companies when Union arrived, the company either bought them out or crushed them. Union Ice fixed prices and gave its drivers cash with which to buy drinks for prospective customers. For decades to come, Union Ice Company drivers were caught in fights with other delivery services.[70] Advertising harped on the purity of natural ice and the impurities of artificial ice, though by the turn of the century, Union Ice had acquired several ice plants in its aggressive expansion and quietly made and delivered clear ice from them.

The results were not favorable for the consumer. In Los Angeles, with the advent of Union Ice, prices climbed from $0.50 for 100 pounds to $1.50, "except to barrooms which are privileged to buy for $1 per 100 pounds, presumably on account of the good work they are engaged in." The "Union Company" is "a trust as wicked and outrageous as if they had cornered breadstuffs and made our poor and hungry people pay fifteen or twenty cents per roll for bread."[71]

By the time Union Ice arrived in Oxnard in 1924, it had been through numerous lawsuits and turf wars and already had a foothold in the neighborhood with a cold storage facility in Ventura. This was a battle it was planning to win.

ICING OXNARD

Ord placed an advertisement in the *Oxnard Daily Courier* next to the news that Union Ice was announcing its plans for a plant. The new Ord plant at one-hundred-tons-daily capacity would dwarf its existing forty-ton plant. The new plant would also house four thousand tons of ice in storage. Ord's first plant had cost $65,000. Ord Ice was spending $100,000 on the second plant.[72] The company started plans and site work immediately.

By mid-May 1924, Union was already building a forty-ton plant. The site Union chose was the W.H. Lathrop property on which Ord had dropped the option less than a year earlier. Union was going to be Ord's immediate neighbor.

The newspapers iced over the coming war, saying there would be plenty of produce to ship out of Oxnard. In June, as the new Union and Ord plants rose, the *Daily Courier* reported that Guadalupe and Salinas "have already made their mark" with summer lettuce, "and this season, Oxnard came to the front with a splendid quality product."[73] A total of "900 carloads will be packed from 1,500 acres. As the vegetable shipments have created such a large demand for ice, the Ord Ice Company is enlarging its plant and the Union Ice Company is building an entirely new one."[74]

Oxnard was just one of the Union Ice Company's battle zones. While the Oxnard plant was under construction in August, the company acquired Pacific Ice's brand-new plant in Dixon, California, a town lying between Vacaville and Sacramento. "The absorption of the Dixon plant leaves Union Ice Company in complete control of the ice situation in [Dixon], and the company is well able to meet all the requirements of the local field with its new $40,000 plant recently completed on the corner of Lincoln Avenue and Sixth Street."[75]

Then Union nailed down the contract for Southern Pacific Railroad icing in Watsonville, California, an area where lettuce had gone from nothing in 1921 to 1,500 projected carloads in 1924.[76]

In October, Union announced aggressive expansion plans in the San Diego area. With two plants already in place, Union started construction on two new plants in late 1924 and promised to build three more in the region in the next year.[77]

In October in Oxnard, Ord Ice had barely finished building its expanded plant when Union started production. Undercutting Ord on price, prime contracts moved down the tracks from Ord to Union. Before the month was out, Ord was done in. Emmett Ord turned to his nemesis in Santa Barbara

Union Ice, Oxnard, California, circa 1950. *Oxnard Public Library.*

over the larger, darker one in Oxnard. Puritan Ice announced the purchase of the Ord Ice Company later that month.[78]

Emmett Ord remained as the manager of Ord Ice in both Santa Barbara and Oxnard. He continued to run the Ord plant and delivery service in Santa Barbara, with his fleet of *Ord—It's Scored—Ice* trucks continuing to make deliveries, but the accounting all went through the newly incorporated Mission Ice Company of Santa Barbara.

Mission Ice was a new Puritan company, formed expressly as an umbrella firm under which it could retain the distinct names and management of the separate Puritan and Ord businesses:

> *Explanation of the interlocking of* [companies] *was found in a plan to form a distributing company which would allow the Ord and Puritan Ice companies to retain their identity under contract to sell all ice to the Mission Ice Company...However, it was stated by interested parties that the articles of incorporation for the Mission Ice company were filed in premature anticipation of developments and that the deal between the* [companies] *is not completed although purchases in Oxnard...have been reported.*[79]

Later reports made it clear the sale was partial. Puritan owned the Santa Barbara and Ventura plants outright, but at Oxnard, possibly due to the sources of original funding, it owned the land, buildings and only a portion of the plant.

While the deal was being sealed—it took almost a year to finalize the purchase—and for two years beyond, the Ord Ice plants in Oxnard and

Ventura continued to operate, though they were largely silent in the typically trumpeting media.[80] Phillips and Dalzell, running Ord as a subsidiary of Mission Ice, may have toyed with the notion of going up against Union Ice. They had a running experiment in the venture at any rate and would have watched the side-by-side Ord and Union ice plants in Oxnard with interest.

In Santa Barbara, Mission Ice increasingly became the local delivery arm of the company, with the Mission Ice logo replacing the Puritan logo on delivery trucks. The company's delivery business at this point covered Santa Barbara, Ventura, Oxnard and Santa Barbara's north county. In 1929, Mission took a more physical form when it opened a separate office two doors down from Ord (located at 209 West Canon Perdido) at 201 West. Lester Quensel, a manager hired away from Santa Barbara Ice, ran the office. (Quensel would later open and operate the City Ice Service on Haley.)

In Oxnard, the operation of Ord Ice Company remained under the Ord name and advertised with a level of desperation and insistence. It was even selling its meltwater.

One advertisement from June 1926 reads, "Ord Ice has been agreeably surprised to have its many friends tell them of the WONDERFUL SOFTNESS of the water from their ice. In fact, many housewives buy Ord ice for a twofold purpose—To save food and later as an Additional Economy in cleaning the skin and hair. A phone call will assure Quick and Efficient Service."[81]

A contest announced June 29, 1926, reminded local residents that Ord Ice was worth as much melted as frozen. On July 23, Ord would place a three-hundred-pound block of ice in the front window of the downtown Oyster Loaf Café and see how long it took to melt. Contestants were to bring their guesses to Ord Ice by July 3. The top three winning tickets would receive ice books of four-, eight- and sixteen-dollar value, respectively. Sixteen dollars bought a ton of ice at retail prices at the time.[82]

Later that same month, Ord general manager M.M. Clarke reported a 90 percent annual increase in business for the company. Clarke "expect[ed] the largest year in the company's history in Oxnard" for 1927.[83]

But the Ords would not enjoy 1927 in Oxnard. In November 1926, Puritan Ice sold "the good will, motor equipment, and part of the refrigerator equipment of the Ord Ice Company's branches in Ventura and Oxnard" to Union Ice.[84]

Union, for its part, now boasted sixty-four ice factories in Southern California. In Ventura County, it reconstructed and then reopened the old Ord plant in Ventura and then poured investment into Oxnard. New

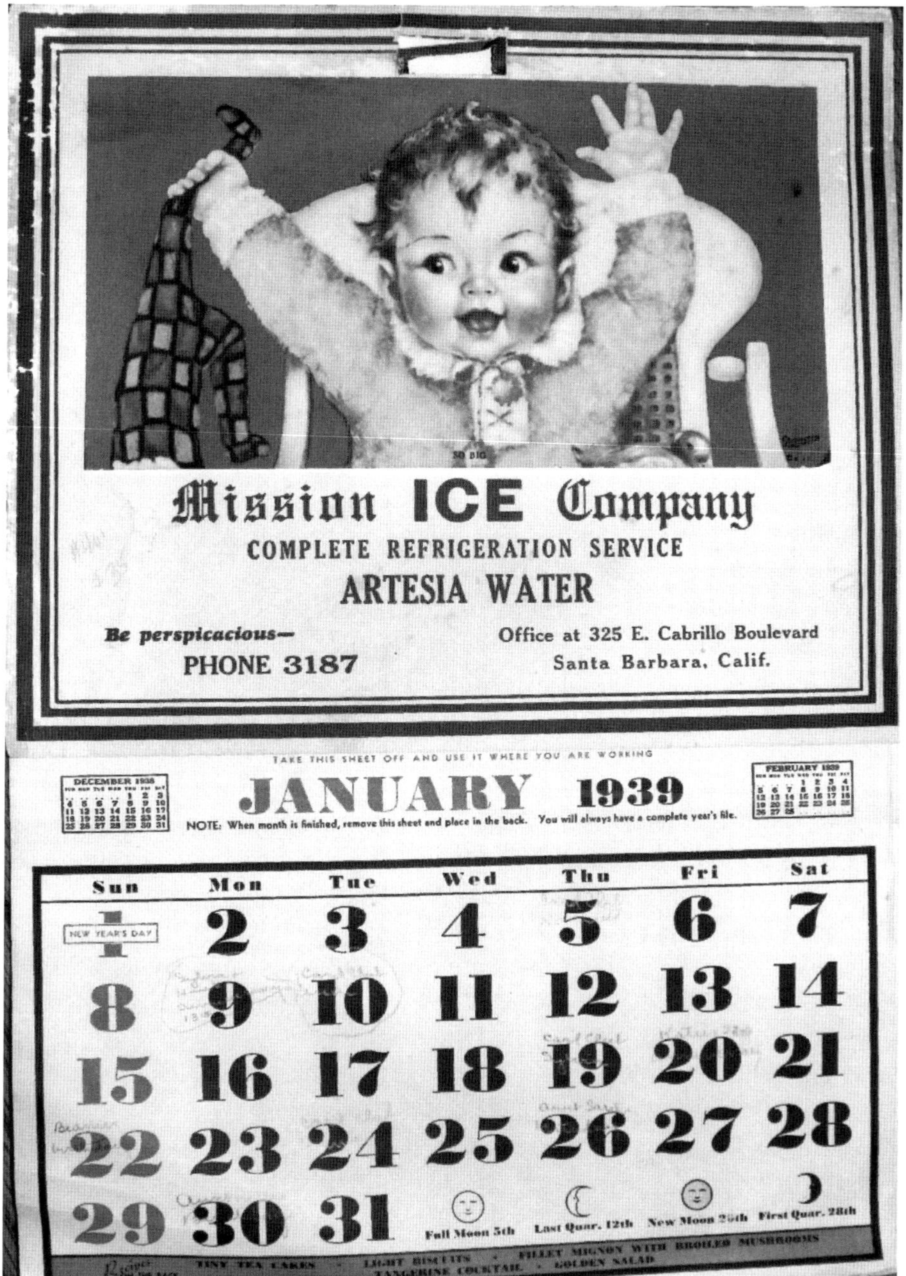

Mission Ice calendar, 1939. Printed by *American Cookery* magazine. *Author's collection.*

manufacturing capacity, new loading platforms for up to twenty-two rail cars at a time, new rail spurs and a new storage facility "entirely airtight so no air can lower the temperature...The walls have seven layers, one board wall, a tar paper, another board wall, then 12 inches of sawdust, and then one board layer, tar paper, another wooden layer, and on the outside, stucco trim. Below the concrete flooring there is a cork-insulated layer."[85] Next on its plans was an upgrade of the Santa Paula plant.

In January 1927, Emmett and son Robert Ord announced that they would dismantle their Santa Barbara plant at 209 Canon Perdido and move portions of the machinery to Los Angeles county, where the two Ords would "personally superintend" a new plant.[86] No word of the plant appears in Los Angeles papers, there was no announcement in *Ice and Refrigeration Annual* and there were no articles of incorporation to commemorate a new Ord Ice plant. The phone directories of the time are also silent.

If one was launched, it was likely Robert Ord's to run. Emmett Ord's residential address remained in Santa Barbara, and Ord Ice retained its offices and delivery fleet under the wing of Mission Ice. City directories at the time listed job titles as well as addresses, and Emmett, living at 824 Bath Street, was listed for a couple years after the Oxnard sale with the figurehead title of "Founder and Manager" of Ord. But in 1931, with Emmett at the age of sixty-six, Ord Ice closed its doors, and Emmett Ord was listed as a salesman for Puritan Ice Company.

The following year, Ord showed no affiliation. His ice career was over.

Puritan Ice remained largely in the shadows during the absorption and dissolution of Ord. It appears only as it reached out and purchased the firm. Even when the sale of the Oxnard facility went through to Union Ice, Puritan officers only appear on the deeds. The newspapers quickly forgot the links between Puritan and Ord, and ice tonnage and farming yields both sunk lower on the news horizon as the problems were solved in a big way. Ord was wicked away like meltwater in a hot sun, and Puritan remained, hidden under the guise of Mission Ice, in Santa Barbara.

To be fair, however, it was during these same years that Puritan Ice was creating an empire of a wholly different sort in Atascadero. In an era of immense poultry popularity, by 1928, Puritan Ice would own and operate the largest poultry ranch in the world.

Chapter 5

Poultry Utopia in Atascadero

In late 1912, Edward Gardner Lewis sent a letter to thousands of supporters, subscribers and former subscribers asking for their support in a new venture. After designing and building a planned residential city, University City outside St. Louis, Missouri, and creating the largest circulation magazine in the United States, *Woman's National Weekly*, with a circulation of 1.6 million, he was quitting and heading west.

He was financially wiped out and exhausted. Both he and his wife, Mabel, were in poor health. He had just concluded five years of legal battles with the United States Postal Service over his magazine's right to use second-class postage. Postmaster George Cortelyou had issued a fraud order against Lewis for using his magazines as a means to raise money for other businesses. The order barred Lewis from using second-class rates, and as a result, his subscriptions had declined.

Over the next seven years, the U.S. Postal Service indicted Lewis fourteen times. But when the case finally reached federal court, the judge threw it out. Congress proposed restitution to Lewis Publishing Company of "the sum of one-million five-hundred thousand dollars for injuries wrongfully inflicted." In later years, Lewis would say, "I did not attempt to obtain the indemnity, as I was now penniless and found that indemnities awarded for claims in connection with the Revolutionary War were still unpaid."[87]

The letter Lewis sent, like most of his missives and publications, sought investors and supporters. This time, the letter requested their help in founding "a great Colony, along entirely new lines, carefully thought

Edward Gardner Lewis, circa 1925. *Atascadero Public Library.*

out, as the result of years of experience in the founding and building up of University City." He asked for a $2-per-acre commitment to create an option fund to finance the new colony. Within a few weeks, he had received 1,700 applications for five- to ten-acre parcels, or something on the order of $20,000 to $30,000. It was enough for a down payment. His vision was of "a city in the country, especially adapted to the automobile, with small orchard estates, residential section and all of the civic, educational and businesses as well as the administrative building grouped into a civic center." In January 1913, the Lewises set off to California with $2,000 in borrowed funds. Given the subscriptions they'd received, he would need twenty thousand acres to make it work.[88]

He made it work in spades.

Within a few short weeks, Lewis was able to locate and purchase Rancho Atascadero. Lewis wrote to his followers:

> *It is in San Luis Obispo County, California, on the main line of the Southern Pacific Railroad, and traversed from end-to-end by the great state highway from Los Angeles to San Francisco and located midway between these, the two great markets of the Pacific Coast. Approximately 23,000 acres in extent, in one vast holding, the soil of the richest sandy loam, abundantly watered, within five miles of a deep sea harbor* [Port San Luis] *and a beautiful sea beach, with a picturesque mountain ridge between it and the ocean, tempering the climate to a delightful blend of sea and mountain air, with an average rainfall for the past 12 years of 26.33 inches, with soil from 10 to 30 feet deep, much of it never scratched by a plow.*[89]

The deed was transferred to Lewis's new organization, the Colony Holding Corporation. He paid $37.50 an acre for the land, a total of $862,500, and promised to pay it off in 120 days.

As new letters of subscription went out, the money rolled in, and Lewis brought in experts from around the country to help him plan, design and build his new and improved ideal city. Architects, city planners, engineers and horticulturalists all converged, and on June 12, 1914, Lewis laid the cornerstone for the City Administration Building. The quote that graces its entry was Lewis's, and it represents him through and through: "Keep your face to the sunshine and you cannot see the shadows."

The vast Rancho Atascadero tract was subdivided in sections and lots as Lewis envisioned. A tent city went up, and lots were sold. While Lewis focused on erecting the admin building, a large printery for his publishing empire and a hospital, homes began to spring up. By 1917, over three hundred residences, both in town and on the orchard estates, had been built and occupied.

Lewis's vision kept the new residents busy and productive. The printery employed scores with his *Woman's National Weekly* and *Woman's Farm Journal*. From Atascadero, he launched his immediately successful *Illustrated Review*, a picture-magazine that was a precursor to *Life* magazine, and which had achieved a circulation of one million by 1917. He also published his view of the University City events with another publication, *The Siege of University City*, by Sydney Morse.[90]

But Lewis's primary vision was of a utopian life close to the land, with a ready market for products and a town center for culture and education and civic participation. The ready markets may have been, as he wrote, San Francisco and Los Angeles, but Lewis was not content leaving livelihood to the residents of his community. Lewis researched and then brought in flower seed contracts, as well as egg and pullet contracts, and then he landed a contract for dehydrated fruits and vegetables from the United States Army for provisioning of American troops fighting World War I in Europe. "A climax in the production and dehydration of vegetables in Atascadero was reached in October of 1918, when Mr. Lewis secured a government contract for 2,250 tons of dehydrated vegetables, which meant the production of 45,000,000 pounds of fresh vegetables. The order came from the Quartermasters' Department of the American Army, in a telegram informing him that the contract had been awarded to Atascadero."[91]

To support the breadth and depth of Lewis's agricultural vision, he created the Caladero Products Company to market, pack and ship the region's agricultural wealth. One of Caladero Products' first needs was a state-of-the-art packing plant.

GAY ENGINEERING BELIEVES IN ATASCADERO

The contract with the army for dehydrated fruits and vegetables was inked in the waning days of World War I. By 1919, the war was over and the troops mostly back home. But the contract remained in force, and Caladero built out an infrastructure to support this and other contracts.

Caladero's focus on a packing plant to support the shipment of dehydrated products quickly widened to include an ice-making and cold storage plant. In early 1922, C.G. Tanner, San Luis Obispo County horticultural commissioner said, "If this [packing] plant is located here, a large cold storage plant would also be constructed here by a cold storage company already having plants in several fruit centers, including Watsonville."

Tanner then raised the competitive bar. "He considered Atascadero the ideal place for the location of the [cold storage] plant, but that Templeton or Paso Robles would also be good locations and that the Templeton people had already made overtures to him. Attention was called to the fact that the Caladero Products Company was putting in a 10-line canning [factory] and would engage in dehydrating also this season."[92]

By April, the headlines read, "Cold Storage Plant Assured." "By the first of July there will be standing in Atascadero one of the finest cold storage plants in California and the only one in this Central Coast Section of the State." The plant was to be financially guaranteed by Caladero Products Company, signatory E.G. Lewis. There would be packing, icing and cold storage for Atascadero's "pear, peach, apricot, cherry, prune, and apple trees and the acres of blackberries, loganberries and strawberries."

A pair of icemen akin to Phillips and Dalzell stepped in to build and operate the plant. W.E. Higman and G.H.M. Dorsey, "who have erected a number of large and modern cold-storage and pre-cooling plants in California," agreed to build a modern ice and cold storage facility. Design and construction were contracted through Gay Engineering, "the largest builders of refrigerating plants on the Pacific Coast, to erect and equip the building for a total cost of $200,000."[93]

Details of the plant promised Atascadero farmers a brighter, more marketable future. The plant would produce up to twenty tons of ice daily. There would be six pre-cooling rooms with a capacity for storing 2,100 crates of produce at thirty-two degrees Fahrenheit. "This will enable every box of fruit sent out from Atascadero to be reduced in temperature to such an extent that it will enter the fruit cars at a very low temperature and will stay there without exhausting the ice in the car to keep it…This pre-cooling method adds many days to the keeping quality of the fruit."

"Rushing uncooled fruit upon the market in quantities beyond the capacity of the market to consume results in low prices and much loss from deterioration of quality," the writer warned. The cold storage unit would extend the life, and therefore the market, for Atascadero produce, well past the brief harvest-to-table timeframe currently available.[94]

Exterior, Puritan Ice, Atascadero, plant #3, circa 1930. *Bruce Phillips collection.*

There would also be an egg-storage room with a capacity of four thousand standard boxes, also at thirty-two degrees Fahrenheit, and a poultry-storage room with space for up to twenty tons of dressed chicken in barrels or crates and a "sharp" freezer room—kept at zero degrees Fahrenheit—twenty by thirty feet and twelve feet tall. The plant would feature a one-hundred-foot loading platform and an icing platform along the rail spur.

The building of the cold storage facility was front-page news in Atascadero.[95] By July 28, 1922, the plant was delivering ice to local residents and icing rail cars under the name of Atascadero Ice and Cold Storage Company. "Ice is now a household necessity and the housewife is realizing what effect a few degrees difference in temperature has upon food."[96]

Not everyone in town was behind the erection of the packing and cold storage plant. It was an investment that would take years to amortize. There were also local grumblings as town father E.G. Lewis shifted his gaze outside the area and began developing oil fields and mines and then launched a concentrated effort at yet another planned development, as he bought up tracts of land near Los Angeles in what he was calling Palos Verdes Estates.

In August 1922, however, the value of the new ice plant was confirmed as railroad strikes flared, shipments across the continent were delayed and California growers in general saw huge losses during a peak season as their produce rotted on sidings.

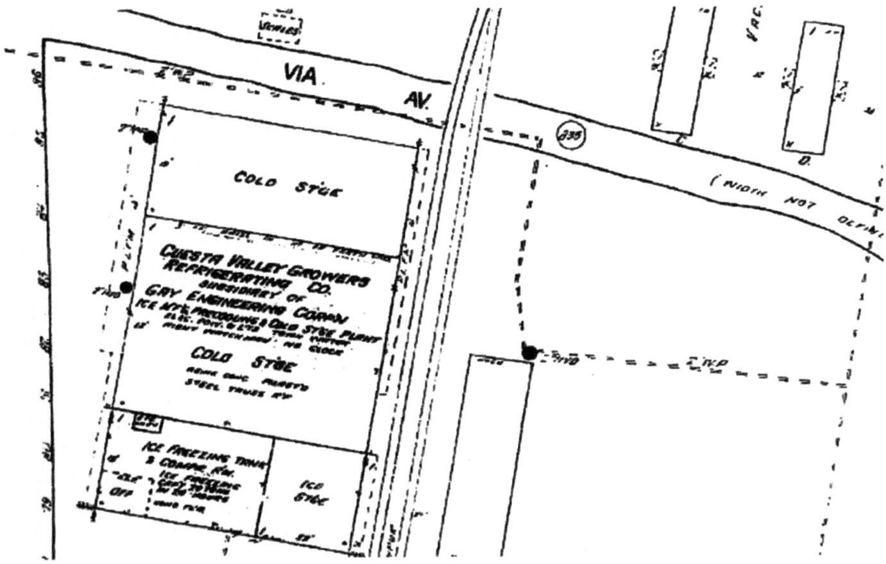

On Atascadero city plat maps, Cuesta Growers is shown as a subsidiary of Gay Engineering. 1926. *Atascadero Public Library.*

> *The present freight tie-up and the tremendous losses fruit growers of California face should cause the orchardists of Atascadero Estates and adjacent regions to realize what a boon to them the large cold storage plant built here in such a hurry this summer is destined to be. If at the same time they also realize that they are in no way responsible for it, but were, most of them, rather a hindrance than a help, it may help also to make them realize the exact situation better and what would now be the situation if one man* [E.G. Lewis] *had not the foresight, the courage and the good will to provide this measure of relief.*[97]

The article appeared on the front page of the *Atascadero News*, a paper Lewis owned and operated. Where he felt his vision outstripped support for implementation, he was quick to defend himself.

R.A. Leigh, manager of Atascadero Fruit Growers' Exchange, attributed the success to the "vision and public spirit of E.G. Lewis in obligating himself for a quarter of a million dollars in order to get it [the plant] and get it this year."[98] By November, it was "safe to say that, had the [cold storage] plant not been in existence, Atascadero would have profited very little from its fruit crop this year, owning to the railroad and coal strikes and difficulty of securing cars."

A year later, in 1923, the United States government dehydration contract was cancelled, and Higman and Dorsey stepped out of the ice business. The plant had been partially financed by Gay Engineering, and it was still holding the trust deed. Gay formed Cuesta Growers, a holding company, to operate the plant in order to recover Gay's construction costs. It was the second plant known to have been owned and operated by Gay, the first being in Palmdale, California. Robert Murray was put in charge of the Atascadero plant, and the business model shifted to providing services for growers outside the immediate region. Space in the plant was rented to the Rivers Brothers Company of Los Angeles to store apples from Soledad and Watsonville. Murray told the paper, "At Palmdale when our growers saw the Eastern market was going 'fluey' they put their pears in cold storage and held them for four months. At the end of that time we sold [the pears] for eight and nine cents per pound on our own Los Angeles market." The ice plant in Atascadero, Murray said, was running at full capacity.[99]

A few weeks later, the plant exceeded its capacity for cooling fruit. "The ice plant has a capacity of 30 tons of ice per day and 50 tons of refrigeration. [However,] the demand for space has made it necessary to press the ice storage room into service for the apples."[100]

A year and a half later, the Lewis magic would disappear, and one of the early casualties would be the ice plant.

The Lewis Snowball Melts

On the morning of December 16, 1924, the fate and future of Atascadero were forever reshaped. E.G. Lewis, working at his desk in the Atascadero City Administration Building, looked up to see "several men accompanied by a United States marshal" approaching. Taken completely by surprise, Lewis was informed that, on the petition of five creditors in the Seattle area whose claims amounted to no more than $8,000, the $20 million Lewis organization was being forced into involuntary bankruptcy.[101]

The assault was carefully planned. Lewis had no inkling, and his thousands of magazine subscribers and investors were informed within days of the action through the illegal use of the Lewis Publishing Company's proprietary mailing lists. The assault was also successful. Severed from access to funds and supporters and caught straddling more than his usual number of large new financial ventures, Lewis toppled.

Lewis quickly formed a Defense and Reconstruction Fund but unwisely focused on reconstruction rather than defense; he funneled the money he raised into his ongoing projects at the time, including oil wells in Maricopa and at Signal Hill in Long Beach, silver mines in Wyoming, a chemical plant in Oakland and the pools of money he was spending to develop Palos Verdes Estates outside Los Angeles.

He was trying desperately to slice off another big success before the debtors could get him into court. This, he believed, would rally his many supporters.

But Lewis was running in front of a fast-growing snowball of commitments. Lewis, in his 1929 autobiography, *E.G. Lewis: Fraud or Friend?*, estimated that his personal indebtedness in the early 1920s had reached $8.5 million.[102]

Within two weeks, over a miserable Christmas season, Lewis folded and admitted defeat, and the faithful investors in the hundreds suddenly became creditors and came forth with their claims.[103] Attorney Oscar Willett, a court-appointed receiver from Seattle, was placed in charge of the Atascadero-based Colony Holdings.[104]

Throughout 1925 and 1926 the preliminary legal wranglings continued with Lewis's accounts on display. A federal trial in September 1927 found Lewis guilty of ten counts of fraudulent use of U.S. Mails (magazine solicitations for funds that were not put to the promised uses) and sentenced him to six years in prison. A second trial in January 1928 found Lewis guilty of fourteen additional counts of fraud and diversion of funds.[105]

Lewis was ultimately fined $14,000 and sentenced to serve fourteen years at McNeil Island Penitentiary, located on the Puget Sound in Washington state. Lewis did not appeal and reported to the gates of the penitentiary on May 1, 1928.

Lewis's closing years remained difficult. He was a model prisoner, becoming close friends with the warden, and he was released on parole in 1931. But returning to Atascadero, he disliked the progress and methods in town, especially of the Atascadero Development Syndicate that Oscar Willett—more on him in a moment—had set up to run things and wrote letters on his viewpoints. The very act of dropping his missives in the mail violated his parole, and he was arrested and returned to McNeil. He was finally released in April 1934. He returned to their Los Angeles family home, where Mabel Lewis died a year later. After her death, he returned to Atascadero and the "Headquarters house" he had lived in during his years there. In 1937, he attempted to market a medicine atomizer with small success. Lewis died August 10, 1950, eighty-one years of age, in Atascadero.

Had the stumbling block not been thrown down by the Seattle creditors, Lewis may have been able to continue his dash ahead of the rolling snowball. However, his indebtedness was huge. Expensive exploratory oil wells in the Taft area had failed on the eve of the attack. And the Great Depression was just down the road. Nevertheless, his achievements were substantive, and because of his downfall, his influence on women's politics, publishing and city design and planning, especially in the realm of economic support for pastoral lifestyles, has remained largely unheralded and unexamined.

During the dark times in Atascadero, people pulled up stakes and left. Crops fell off. Demand for ice plummeted.

WILLETT WILLS A FUTURE

Starting in 1925, attorney Oscar Willett, the court-appointed receiver representing the disgruntled Seattle creditors, began to sell assets and clear the books of the Colony Holding Corporation of debt and bankruptcy. By September, a single issue of the *Atascadero News* would run six front-page stories about Willett. Centered on page one, under the heading of "He Does Things!," Willett was given the mantle of veneration that Lewis formerly wore. "Every week should be Jubilee Week in Atascadero for not one passes but Oscar L. Willett launches or puts over one or more major projects for Atascadero."[106]

During the week, he had opened the First National Bank in town—first-day deposits were $70,000—and completed the bankruptcy proceedings for the Colony Holding Corp., sending a score or more of bankruptcy attorneys packing. The printery had been sold and kept functioning, keeping precious local jobs. He was managing a Real Estate Settlement Plan, assigning over $10 million of debt by this time. He also launched the Vineyard and Poultry Syndicate to support the development of the wine industry and poultry ranches.

It was in this wind of change that Puritan Ice Company came to town. In May 1926, with the cold storage plant almost dormant at this point, the paper announced that "Dalzell and Phillips, owners of controlling interest in the Puritan Ice Company of Santa Barbara and of the ice and storage plant at Santa Maria [Guadalupe], have arranged to purchase the Cuesta Valley Ice Company of Atascadero."[107]

Phillips and Dalzell committed to an immediate $250,000 investment in reopening and refurbishing the facility, "exercising an option they have held for some time."

The Puritan story by now was a solid business tale and worth telling. "Dalzell & Phillips, although primarily interested in cold storage plants, have always maintained a policy of providing their company with sufficient produce to insure [*sic*] its continued operation. When they entered the Santa Maria field, there was not a single carload of perishable freight moved out of that city. Dalzell & Phillips immediately planted 1,000 acres of lettuce to point the way and encourage all residents to do likewise."

It was pears that were the big success to date in Atascadero.

Soon after taking over and "realizing the expectations of Puritan Ice Company," twelve carloads of pears were stored in the pre-cooling rooms of the plant, the greatest number in its history. Atascadero pears had been shipped to Manila in the Philippines a week prior. "Atascadero will furnish a good percentage [of the pears] for the 'Sparkle' brand, the best shipped by the [Colony Holding] company."[108]

The slow months at the plant, with earlier misgivings over building it in the first place, fed a continuing culture of complaint about the plant. Newly hired manager D.J. Chamberlain set out to convince farmers of the effectiveness of the plant for what was Atascadero's primary export crop for 1926. Chamberlain staged a public display that, as with all things ice, ended up on the front page of the paper. "The box of firm, juicy, rosy-cheeked pears that has been exhibited by the Puritan Ice Company in Vail's [grocery store] show window for the past two weeks has been a source of surprise to many who have been skeptical as to the advantages of cold storage for fruit. The idea has been more or less prevalent the pears would keep only a short time in cold storage and would rot very quickly after being taken out, but the pears displayed were placed in cold storage at the Ice Company's plant July 20 and taken out in perfect condition December 6. They are still in good shape [on December 26] for marketing."[109]

But pears were not the product Puritan chose to create the ice and cold storage demand for its latest ice plant. Seeing down the line of Edward Lewis's earlier vision, it determined to launch a sizable poultry ranch. "Terms of the agreement with Mr. Willet required the new company to have the first 10,000 hen poultry unit built and ready for operation by January 1."[110]

Puritan acquired one hundred acres of a large block of land at the far northwest corner of Rancho Atascadero and hired California's top chicken man to run its operation.

Chicken Man

Ralph Barrows Easson wrote the book on chickens. Released in March 1923, *California Poultry Production* was the essence of five years of experience traversing the state as the University of California's Agricultural Extension instructor in poultry husbandry.[111] The 175-page book covered the gamut, with chapters on "Factors Influencing Profits in the Poultry Industry," "Poultry Housing," "Breeding," "Feeding," "Natural and Artificial Incubation," "Brooding," "Marketing," "Poultry Records and Accounts," "Turkeys," "Ducks" and "Diseases and Parasites."

Easson's writing, like the courses and workshops he offered up and down the state, was lucid and straightforward. "The male suited to head any breeding flock must have many qualifications. It is as necessary for him to have vigor and vitality as it is that pullets and hens should be selected for these characteristics. The male should come from trap-nested stock with good production records back of him. He should be pedigreed so that his exact ancestry is known; the longer the pedigree, the better. That he comes from a pen of high producers is not enough; he must be capable of transmitting high egg production characteristics to his daughters."[112]

Easson was widely known in the state for his culling workshops. He would arrive in a town—Van Nuys, Fresno, San Bernardino, El Centro, Redlands, Ventura and Atascadero to name a few—with plenty of notice and travel to two or three poultry ranches in a day with a group of thirty to fifty poultry ranchers following behind. At each, he would cull the flocks, taking the gathered farmers through the steps and staying in each town for three to seven days.

Culling a flock was a process of selecting higher-producing birds over lower-producing ones and getting rid of the underperformers in the form of dressed chickens for the market.

Idyllic view of the Puritan Poultry farm, circa 1929. *Author's collection.*

In Van Nuys, Easson explained to the group (and the paper faithfully printed), "Many hens which cease laying during the summer, will produce no more eggs until December, so only the high producers will be carried through the expensive moulting season."[113] In Ventura, he told the ranchers to cut their flocks by a third each year. "Feeding only ⅔ of a flock and getting nearly 100 percent of the eggs cuts down the cost per dozen eggs surprisingly."[114] In Woodland, near Sacramento, he hammered the lesson home: "Twenty percent of [your] flock are non-paying boarders."[115]

The means of identifying the good layers was sharply delineated. Producers attributes were, in order: vitality good, late moulters, pale vents, pale shanks, pale beaks, pale earlobes, pale skin, flexible pelvic bones, full red waxy combs, good body capacity and good condition.

Birds that wanted culling molted early. They had yellow vents and shanks, their combs were shriveled and they had a small body capacity.[116]

Easson's culling example, 1929. *Author's collection.*

Road-weary, he may also have wanted to show what could really be done with a poultry ranch. Phillips and Dalzell were the perfect partners for such a scheme. As in Guadalupe when they hired Raymond Ellis—more on Ellis when we return to Guadalupe—they looked for experts to build up the businesses that would feed their core business: ice. Easson's book was the bible in the field, and so they took the mountain to Mohammed.

The combination was an unusual one. The *Los Angeles Times* found it incongruous: "It may seem a far cry from ice to poultry, but there is a logical connection which the Puritan Ice Company of Santa Barbara, Guadalupe, and Atascadero, saw. With an ice and packing concern in operation, it wanted eggs in quantities, and to further this desire it formed the Puritan Poultry Corporation."[117]

The new poultry farm opened on the third week in August 1926, and on October 3, the first batches of baby chicks were moved into the houses. By the close of the year, eight thousand White Leghorn baby chicks were hatched under twenty electric brooders. The chicken houses were of the University type, which meant they were gabled and deep rather than shed-like and shallow. Four units were built at first, 250 feet long, with room for ten thousand laying hens. "A 15,000-egg electric incubator has been installed and hatching begins in earnest this month." And "in the centrally-located feed house the electrically operated grinding and mixing machine has a capacity of a ton of material. The green feed is chopped electrically. An overhead carrier system leading from the feed house to the four laying houses brings the feed conveniently to the birds and carries away the litter."

The eggs sold well. The pullets sold well. Almost immediately, Puritan announced plans for growth. "Mr. Dalzell of the Puritan Ice Company who visited the plant last week, prophesied that it would be only a short time now before the big cold storage rooms would be filled to capacity with eggs and poultry alone, judging by the way they are coming in." Puritan will "increase its plant from 10,000 [hens] to either 30,000 or 50,000 during 1927, Mr. Dalzell told Mr. Willett during a conference last week."[118]

For his part, Oscar Willett, who was now the full-time "Father of Atascadero," got caught up in the excitement of it. "Willett has announced that he will build a 10,000-hen plant this year on the open runway plan so that visitors can see the two Atascadero types in action on the one tract. This will give [Willet's Atascadero Development] Syndicate a capacity of 16,000 hens."

Dalzell was talking up their great chicken venture in Santa Barbara, as well, and convinced Charles C. Witmer to invest in the venture. Witmer, two

Puritan Poultry egg crate label, circa 1929. *Bruce Phillips collection.*

years younger than the Puritan partners, was a famous and early aviator. A graduate in 1911 from the first class of Glenn Hammond Curtiss's Curtiss School of Aviation at North Island near San Diego, he held the fourth pilot's license issued in the state of California and the fifty-second for the United States. Witmer had turned to building dirigibles through his company, Airships, Inc., of Hammondsport, New York, and by the late 1920s was simply known as a capitalist.

But chickens took his fancy, and he not only invested directly in Puritan but also bought property across the road from the Puritan Poultry ranch and started his own ranch. Witmer erected a 5,000-chicken ranch in early February and announced plans to expand to 40,000 almost immediately.[119] Across the road, Puritan was projecting growth to 100,000 birds. The largest chicken ranch on the planet at the time held approximately 65,000 birds and was located in Texas.[120]

Most Chickens in One Place on the Planet

The remainder of 1927 was a race between Willetts's Atascadero Development Syndicate, Witmer's ranch and Puritan Poultry for bragging rights for the most chickens. But it was clear from the start that Phillips and Dalzell had the larger vision, the stronger commitment and the right manager.

Easson's plans rolled out with scientific precision. He knew exactly how many hens one worker could support. His henhouses were closer to self-sustaining than others with dropping boards to clear the waste and automated feed chutes delivering carefully calculated mixes to his birds.

In March, Easson won the prestigious contract to supply five thousand roosters to the Must-Hatch Incubator Company of Petaluma. The contract required yet larger purchases of chicks to feed the incubators, but Puritan simply kept the pullets, ensuring the plant a large breeding stock for the year ahead.[121] To support the growth, Easson bought more land, acquiring abutting parcels in five- to fifteen-acre chunks. By July, Easson had announced plans for twenty new chicken houses to be built.

In June 1927, the San Luis Farm League visited Atascadero en masse. Puritan's amazing plant was the focal stop on its tour. "The tour then proceeded to the plant of Puritan Poultry Company where manager R.B. Easson gave an interesting address…At present time [the plant] requires 400 tons of barley, 150 tons of wheat, 150 tons of corn, 50 tons of ground wheat, 100 tons of fish meal, 30 tons of bone meal, 5 tons of oyster shells, 2 tons of salt, and 25 tons of alfalfa leaves a year."[122] State officials came to visit in July. "Poultry plants of Atascadero Development Syndicate and Puritan Poultry Corporation are among the best-equipped plants in the state R.H. McDrew, director of field service for Central California Poultry Producers Association declared at the weekly Business Men's luncheon Wednesday noon."[123]

All of this occurred during a slow year for poultry. Easson was quoted regularly in the local paper and in the *Los Angeles Times*. He counseled that his success was easily replicated. "'Now is the time to enter the poultry business to share in the high prices which are certain to follow the low 1927 market,' R.B. Easson, manager of Puritan Poultry Company declared this week."[124]

Puritan Poultry's growth did not stop, and the enthusiasm did not die down. In September, Puritan predicted it would hatch 250,000 chicks in the coming season.[125] By June of the next year, there were the equivalent of fifteen rail car loads of eggs (2.7 million eggs) in cold storage at the Puritan Ice Company in town.[126] There were now 80,000 layers at the Puritan

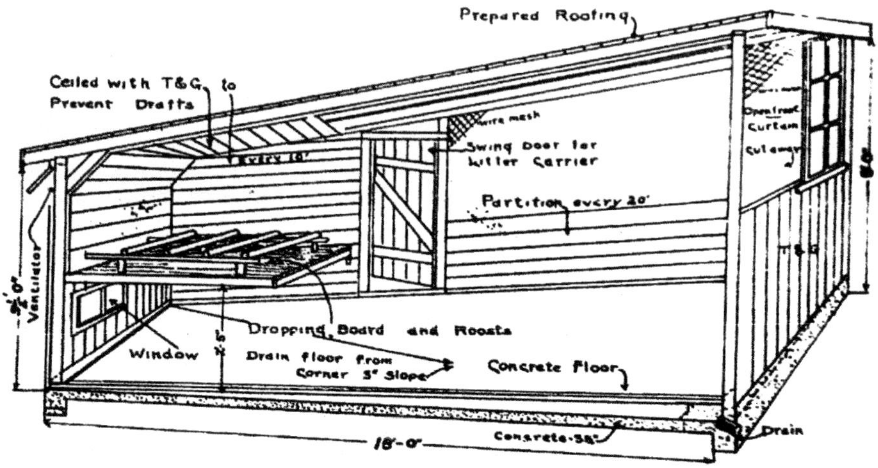

An Easson-designed chicken house on the University plan, circa 1929. *Author's collection.*

Poultry Company ranch. A company brochure touted, "This is by far the largest chicken ranch in the world."[127]

In late June 1928, Dalzell rolled into town for a rare banquet and public pronouncement. "The future of Atascadero can be exactly what you want it to be. All that is needed is absolute loyalty and co-operation with each individual doing his own job well—and a lot of good hard work on the part of all…The first two years of work at Atascadero are just beginning to show and I am personally convinced that Atascadero is on the eve of a great, history-making epoch." The article covering the event said, "Dalzell shattered the 'over-production bugaboo,' by declaring that 'never in the history of the world was there an over-production of quality. Over-production is always encountered in mediocre products.'"[128]

In the meantime, the plant was shipping pears and lettuce by the carload. Growers were storing grapes and grape juice while they waited for markets to rebound. Phillips and Dalzell, ever willing to take on new trappings to achieve new markets, launched Pacific Produce, "a new marketing organization…in Atascadero at the Puritan Ice Plant. T.P. Dalzell and L.R. Phillips, controlling stockholders of Puritan Ice Company, will hold the majority interest in the new company and will use it to build up a larger business for their storage plant at Atascadero." Jack Sisler was named manager, his firm Growers Service Company of Visalia was bought out and merged with the new Puritan Produce. Branch offices were opened in Paso

Robles and San Luis Obispo; the Paso Robles branch was formed by buying out Pelton's Feed Store. "Arrangements are now underway to open a branch in Santa Barbara for the sale and distribution of products."[129]

Atascadero was feeling pretty damned good, too. In January 1928, Oscar Willetts could announce that after selling the hospital, the printery and the City Administration Building, "every business and every building in the civic center proper is now completely out of debt."[130] The *Los Angeles Times* would tie the recovery directly to the influence of Puritan Ice and Puritan Poultry with a headline reading, "That Livid 'Black Eye' That Atascadero Wore Is Fading Under an Egg and Fruit Treatment."[131]

The writer recounted the darker days:

> *Since the days of the ill-starred community project conceived by E.G. Lewis, there have been well-laid streets, rather impressive buildings, and some attractive homes to mark the town. Unfortunately, for a number of reasons, the promised prosperity did not come to the people who bought property and joined the community, and abandoned orchards and forlorn-looking little homes told all too plainly of the failure of its original development program…From the many poultry plants in sight, it is at once evident that the leading industry of the place is egg production. At the present time there are over a quarter of a million birds in the district…It is far from easy for any place which has passed through a period of "the dumps" such as this one experienced, to "come back." It is not easy to overcome prejudice once created.*[132]

The article appeared on October 27, 1929. It was a time of hope and prosperity. Herbert Hoover had taken office in January 1929. His campaign slogan had been, "A chicken in every pot and a car in every garage." Two days after the article about Atascadero's rebirth appeared, the stock market lost a quarter of its value in a matter of hours.

Back in the Dumps

Easson kept a brave face on things through the early 1930s, but a man as expert as he was at the accounting of poultry must have known early that there would be far fewer chickens in pots than Hoover had promised. Unemployment tripled within the year, and the demand (and then the prices) for eggs and chickens fell.

The *Los Angeles Times*, looking for silver linings to print, found a headline in Atascadero, a year after Black Thursday: "Easson Sees Good Future for Poultry." "His statement comes during a time when the poultry business has suffered with all the other industries in the economic depression which has swept through the country." Puritan Poultry Company, Easson continued, "plans an even greater storage of eggs next season when those who lost out this year are frightened out of the field." Egg prices in New York were still high, at fifty-five cents a carton; in Los Angeles, they were selling for forty-one cents.[133]

By the end of the year, the average price for a dozen eggs would drop over 30 percent to thirty-five cents and would keep dropping, until 1933, when eggs would reach twenty-eight cents a dozen.

The remaining Depression years would be a quiet struggle, but by 1935, Ralph Barrows Easson, the man who put California poultry on the map, and especially the Puritan Poultry plant of Atascadero, would be doling out government checks to California's rice farmers for soil conservation measures. In the program, administered through Easson's former and again employer, the University of California Agricultural Extension, Easson visited the rice farms in various locales in Northern California. In each, the farmers filed declarations of their acreages in the soil conservation program. To participate, growers had to have 25 percent of their acreage in soil-conserving crops, which basically meant the acreage had to be idle rice lands. Easson was once again identified as an extension professor and as the Northern California director for soil conservation.[134]

Easson shifted to a desk job in the early 1940s, taking a position as agricultural advisor in the California State Department of Finance. For the remainder of his career, he oversaw the production of agricultural operations at state institutions.[135]

Puritan Poultry stayed in business for six more years. Then, in 1941, with egg prices on the rise again, Puritan Poultry sold its land, the overseer's house, the improvements and its chickens to Kimber Farms, a competitor based in Niles, California, near Oakland.[136] By this time, the Puritan farm was down to twenty-five thousand birds.

For many reasons, which will get full treatment in later chapters, Puritan Ice saw its business in Atascadero melt away over the next decade. In 1953, Puritan quietly transferred ownership of the Atascadero ice plant to Antone

Left: President Herbert Hoover, 1931. *Santa Barbara Public Library.*

Below: Kimber Farms chicken ranch in Atascadero, the former Puritan Poultry ranch. Photo by Walter Hughes. 1957. *Kimber Farms, Inc.*

Ruso, who continued to operate the plant as a local ice delivery service, but fitfully. Puritan would carry the paper on the property, and Ruso would twice, in 1957 and 1959, default on his loan payments.

What happened to Puritan's poultry empire is clouded. The media trumpeted the new and the successful, in large part because the people involved trumpeted themselves, then as now. The struggling, the failing and the failed tend to appear in the county record books only after the fact. But Puritan's end in Atascadero was by no means the end of Puritan in San Luis Obispo County or the end of Puritan as a business. Phillips and Dalzell had surprising tendrils in surprising places.

Next stop, Lompoc.

Chapter 6

Ice in the Fields of Lompoc

Lompoc was a natural extension of the Puritan Ice Company's foothold in Guadalupe. When Puritan arrived in town in the mid-1920s, many of the same Japanese farmers it worked with in Guadalupe leased fields in Lompoc, and the Southern Pacific, with a line in place to the local diatomaceous earth mines, was soon laying a spur to the Puritan site as the region went through one of the area's quicksilver shifts in economic base. Vegetables in quickly expanding truck farms took a place in the local economy along with English mustard, flower seeds and diatomaceous earth. Cut flowers would come later, spreading over former vegetable fields with their higher profits.

But vegetables, when the fields were first tilled for the new crops, were the great new export that would help make Lompoc, or Puritan's vision of Lompoc, a place on the map.

Puritan bought land for its ice plant in Lompoc in 1926. Dalzell and Phillips drove out and surveyed the terrain on one of their trips between Santa Barbara and Guadalupe. In August, they purchased a lot a half block off the existing Southern Pacific line "along a portion of Laurel Ave between O Street and 13th Road." (Thirteenth is now V Street.) The purchase was composed of Town Blocks 267, 268 and 269. Located at 1195 West Laurel, the prior owners were "H.H. Howerton and wife."[137]

No plant was started until late 1929, however. Instead, Puritan worked with Southern Pacific to complete the spur up to, and onto, its new property, and it built a simple loading platform. At first, vegetables grown in the Lompoc

Valley were shipped either to Guadalupe, thirty minutes to the north, for icing or to Santa Barbara, an hour south. A short time later, "the ice used here in vegetable packing [was] shipped in by rail from Guadalupe."[138]

Local fields were not producing at a rate that demanded an ice plant. Not yet.

FIELDS OF IDEALS

Lompoc, California, started out like Atascadero to the north and Summerland to the south as a planned community with at least some trappings of utopia. Atascadero's vision fizzled when E.G. Lewis could not stay ahead of the indebtedness he'd accumulated. Summerland's idyllic spiritualist days (and its spiritualist founder, Henry Lafayette Williams) succumbed to the lure of oil and gas wells on the beach. Lompoc's utopia was less grandiose and, perhaps because of this, more successful. The town was started in 1874 as a temperance town, 46,500 acres split into lots, with deeds printed up outlawing the sale of spirits on either commercial or residential lots.

W.W. Broughton was the visionary town founder. Traveling south from Santa Cruz, where he ran a newspaper, he was looking for a place where he could escape the loose and criminal activities he associated with intemperate drinking, a place where he could raise his family in peace. According to his grandson, Amos Washington Broughton, grandpa W.W. "owned five [different] newspapers. The first was the *Tombstone* [Arizona] *Epitaph*. They kicked him out…because he was a teetotaler."[139]

Passing through the Lompoc Valley, at that time an undeveloped rancho owned by Thomas Dibblee and William Welles Hollister of Santa Barbara, he saw what he wanted: rich farmland, abundant water and a temperate climate. The only structures were the ruins of the old 1787 adobe-brick Mission La Purisima, rattled down by the December 1812 earthquake and left to decay. The new mission was sited four miles to the northwest in *La Cañada de los Berros*, the "Canyon of the Watercress," where there was a better water supply, a more protected site and closer and safer access to the main road through California at the time, El Camino Real.

Broughton quickly organized one hundred California farmers and businessmen into an affiliation called the Lompoc Valley Land Company and, among them, raised $500,000 to purchase the 46,500 acres of the

Lompoc and Mission Veija de la Purisima Ranchos. Broughton completed the transaction October 19, 1874.

The Lompoc Valley Land Company laid out the central township and nearby acreage in varying sized lots. Plans included sites for commercial zones, schools, churches, fraternal organizations and a graveyard. A sale date was set, and Broughton placed ads in papers up and down the California coast, making it clear that Lompoc was to be a temperance town. Now he would see whether his vision was one shared by others.

Tempering

The founding of Lompoc as a temperance town dovetailed with the wider course of anti-drinking sentiment in the United States. Temperance first flowered in the United States, as one would expect, from the pulpit. In the 1830s and '40s, preachers like former drunkard John Bartholomew Gough carpet-bagged across New England preaching a convincing pledge of abstinence.[140] The abstinent soon formed leagues and associations, some of which became international in scope.

As soon as there were leagues, there were demands for legal constraints on the sale and intake of "intoxicating spirits." The attempts to codify these constraints culminated in the Eighteenth Amendment to the United States Constitution: Prohibition. Passed in 1919, the amendment was repealed fourteen years later by the Twenty-first Amendment.

But the line between sanity and the sin of spirits was sharply drawn starting in the mid-1800s. License laws were passed in the early 1860s that forced distillers and purveyors to obtain a liquor license for the first time; some of those laws assigned any damages caused by a drinker to the seller of the spirits. This was thought to be the right and best solution for the control of alcohol and the criminal activity that appeared to go hand-in-glove with it.

One of the more influential license laws was the 1873 Baxter Bill of Indiana. Drafted by Indiana state senator Reverend Nathan T. Batts, "a man of intelligence and influence," the "bill [was] intended to prohibit the sale of intoxicating liquors and to make the liquor seller, as also the owner of the building, responsible for damage done by the sale."[141] The bill went through

W.W. Broughton, founder of Lompoc, circa 1880. *Lompoc Historical Society.*

Senator William Baxter's subcommittee and received a favorable stamp of approval and Baxter's name rather than Batts's.

Temperance activists tracked its results closely. The Massachusetts Temperance Alliance compared the more liberal and typically poorly enforced license laws on the books to the Baxter Bill. In its 1874 annual report, it wrote:

> *Facts and not fancy…demonstrate, that under a* [supposedly] *"judicious and well regulated license law," the manufacture of liquor increased twelve times faster than the increase in population; and with that immense increase, insanity and idiocy doubled, pauperism increased six times, and crime nine times faster than the increase of polls* [the number of voting residents]*; whereas, under the Baxter law, in less than one year, the number of saloons decreased 30 per cent., and crime 28 per cent., although the polls increased 4,000.*[142]

The authors failed to provide their means of measuring pauperism, insanity and idiocy.

Foreshadowing the fate of the Eighteenth Amendment, the particular bubble of hope and possibility represented by the Baxter Bill was popped quickly. The Baxter Bill proved to be unenforceable in court and was repealed by the Indiana State Supreme Court in 1875.

But where the federal and state courts could not always find secure legal footing for licensing establishments that sold alcohol, a township could write its own laws. One of the first in America, and the one Lompoc's founding father W.W. Broughton used as his guide, was Vineland, New Jersey. Founded in 1862 by Charles K. Landis, the town laws initially banned the sale of alcohol and attracted a steadily growing population.

A Vineland report from the early 1870s bragged, "The town expends more money for schools than the whole county did twelve years ago. There is no 'lock-up,' jail, house of correction, court, police or fire department in the town. Having no grog-shops, none of these agencies are needed. Last year there were twenty arrests for trivial causes, and one conviction in the county court from this township."[143]

Temperance, from the pulpit to the legislative bench, was popular. Vineland attracted a growing population and national attention. But Vineland was located in a much more populated region where people had more choices of where to reside and conduct business. Nevertheless, Broughton was not going to sugarcoat his vision for temperance. Before the first lot was sold, the Lompoc bylaws stated, "No vinous, malt, spirituous or other intoxicating liquors shall ever be manufactured or sold upon any portion of the Lompoc and Mission Vieja Ranchos purchased by this corporation."[144] Every deed also contained a clause prohibiting the sale or manufacture of liquor.

It worked. According to a write-up of the time by the Lompoc Historical Society, "A land rush ensued with fierce bidding forcing land prices to skyrocket in just one day."[145] Within a year, there were over two hundred families in the little town. There was a post office, school was in session, a stage passed through three days a week, Broughton had his newspaper circulating and advertising upcoming land sales, and an agricultural college was planned in town, as was a wharf at Surf, nine miles to the west on the coast.[146]

However, when Lompoc incorporated as a town fourteen years later, the state courts nullified the town's temperance provisions, and alcohol slowly leaked in. Fourteen would be the same number of years Prohibition would run forty years later.

Growth Industries

From the valley's earliest settlements, the region was provident and plentiful. Several successive native cultures encamped in the area, each resulting in a shift in diet and, therefore, a shift in tools, generally enabling the hunting of larger game.[147] The last, the Canalino period, saw the significant cultural and material development of the native society. A transitional era followed that began with Captain Juan Cabrillo's first contact with the Chumash in 1542 and ended with the passage of the Gaspar de Portola land expedition that passed west of Lompoc along the coast in 1769.

Then the Spanish slipped more permanently into the valley in 1787 with the founding of the La Purisima Mission, originally sited next to the Chumash village site of *Lompo*. While at least one source translates *Lompo* as "Stagnant Water," the Chumash word is believed to be closer to "Where the Water Breaks Through" or "Land of Many Lakes." The Spanish called it *Lumpoco*.

The Chumash were, like their ancestors and forerunners in the area, hunter-gatherers. They harvested reeds and seeds and made a mainstay of the protein-rich valley oak acorn in their diets. Game included deer, bear, turkey, fish and small game. When the Spanish padres settled the mission, they planted beans, wheat, barley, vineyards and pear orchards.[148]

After settlement of the valley by Broughton's Lompoc Valley Land Company in 1874, the town suffered one pitfall after another—drought, a succession of expensive wharves at Surf washing away and a devastating diptheria epidemic—but many families believed and persisted in Lompoc and eventually prospered.[149]

The newcomers replaced the pear orchards with apples, cherries and walnuts and made butter and cheese. The area produce was trundled in carts first to the Point Sal wharf near Guadalupe and then to wharves built along the coast near the town of Surf.

While exports of local produce began to bolster the economy, the first real agricultural industry of the valley was English mustard. Introduced by J.P. Ball in 1880, the variety grew so prolifically in the valley that Lompoc soon led the world in mustard production. Over twenty-six million pounds of mustard seed were shipped from the Lompoc's Surf wharf in 1886. By 1933, an average of more than thirty-five million pounds of seed was produced annually in the valley. For many years, Lompoc produced as much as 90 percent of the mustard seed grown in the United States. During World War I, Lompoc mustard was used in the manufacture of deadly mustard gas.[150]

Then the Balaam family discovered a massive deposit of diatomaceous earth on their Miguelito Canyon property in 1896. Essentially an accumulation of fossilized single-celled marine algae called diatoms, the dead critters' exoskeletons formed a fine white powdery deposit. At the time, diatomaceous earth was used to stabilize dynamite, filter water, as a mild abrasive for facial scrubs and toothpastes and as a pest control. Later uses evolved including DNA purification and as a growing medium for hydroponics. The open pit mines on the old Balaam tract are still active today, owned and operated by the Johns-Manville Corporation.[151]

Following the turn of the century, as the infrastructure improved and the town stabilized, the outlook for Lompoc's produce began to look up. A state agricultural report noted in 1903, "Lompoc seems the natural home to the apple, and its product has taken the first prize at the great fair at New Orleans, and at Chicago was awarded a diploma of excellence. The codling moth is here unknown, and Lompoc apples are never 'wormy,' so there is every prospect that this industry will eventually become of the first importance, especially as the demand for Lompoc apples always outruns the supply."[152]

This was spoken too soon, however, as the codling moth found its way to Lompoc and soon after decimated the apple and walnut industries.

The next industry followed directly on the heels of this devastating loss. Lompoc had been invested in flowers and flower seeds for some time. Lompoc held its first flower festival in 1898. But it was not until 1907 that the industry got a huge push, when John Smith, a Scotsman familiar with the trials associated with growing sweet peas in the damp climate of the British Isles, arrived in the valley. He convinced local bean farmer Robert D. Rennie to try growing the fickle peas. Rennie planted just half an acre, but that half acre was robust and caught the eye of a seed buyer from the W. Atlee Burpee Seed Company. In turn, W. Atlee Burpee himself learned of the crop and soon arrived by train to investigate the town. Before he left, there were hundreds of acres designated for a profitable new crop of sweet peas.[153]

Burpee declared Lompoc one of only three ideal flower-growing regions in the western world. The other two areas were in Germany and France. They each had the advantage of long years of experience and reputation. Lompoc competed against these sources for the next twenty years, but World War I all but wiped Europe off the flower seed market, so that by 1926, the *Los Angeles Times* reported that in flower seeds, Lompoc "pretty nearly supplies the entire world."[154]

Burpee Seeds Farm Annual, 1909. A Lompoc sweet pea is depicted on the cover. *Lompoc Historical Society.*

In the fields between the sweet-smelling flowers and the acrid mustard, farmers grew potatoes, beans, sugar beets, onions, wheat, barley and corn. Carrots, lettuce, cauliflower, celery and broccoli soon followed. The cool climate of the lower valley and the fertile soil, twenty feet deep in some places, provided perfect conditions for almost any crop. The only limitation was transportation: produce left the valley by ship and truck, using a method called dry shipping. In other words, without ice.[155]

Riding the Bear

Puritan saw its fortunes dip with the stock market crash of October 1929. But after mid-November 1929, things were already looking up. The Dow Jones Industrial had peaked in early September at 381. Stocks fell from that point to below 300 by late October. Then, on October 28 and 29, Black Tuesday, the Dow Jones lost 68 points in two days. The slide continued into November, until on Wednesday, November 13, the market dropped to 198.

But that was the bottom. Or at least *a* bottom. Following this, a market rally occurred that gave many hope that the severe economic hit had been a dip and not a trough. The market started to climb through late November and did not stop until April 1930, when it hit 294. Phillips and Dalzell climbed aboard this bear market and poured some cash into Lompoc.

They announced their intentions like they had in every other town where they built a plant. The December 20, 1930 edition of the *Lompoc Record* blared on the front page, "PURITAN ICE COMPANY $85,000 Program Here."

The article detailed the plans. Construction was beginning at once on a plant that would produce fifty tons of ice a day by the end of January. The plant sounded very much like Puritan's other plants but with telling omissions. "The building will include a compressor room, where the bulk of the machinery will be installed; a tank room where the freezing will be done, and a day storage room. There will be an ice loading platform, and the plans will allow completion of a winter storage warehouse adjoining the day storage plant."[156]

Missing was the raised rail car icing platform. This plant would be used to pack vegetables with ice, load the rail cars with the iced vegetables and blow yet more ice over the crates with a mechanized ice shredder. A later article

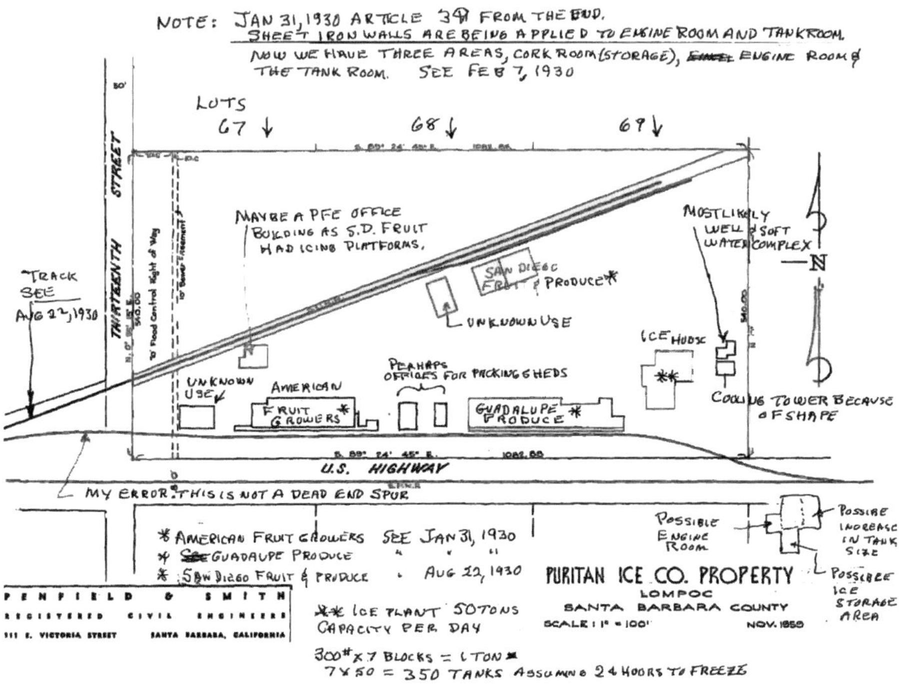

Above: Plat map of Puritan Ice, Lompoc, at the time of Puritan's sale of the property in November 1959. Notes added. *Lompoc Historical Society.*

Left: Guadalupe Produce Lompoc Lettuce label, circa 1931. *John Perry collection.*

described the process. Lettuce "crates [are] filled with oil paper and liberal shovels full of ground ice are mixed with the lettuce. Into the refrigerator cars the freshly iced crates are packed. Plenty of ice is added in order that the lettuce may reach eastern destinations in first class condition. When the car is loaded, a giant blower is brought into operation and ground ice is blown into every possible remaining space in the car."[157]

What the company was not doing was packing ice bunkers on railroad cars from an ice platform above the cars as it was doing in Guadalupe and Santa Barbara.

Also, unlike the Santa Barbara plant, which made both clear and white ice, or Guadalupe, which made only white ice, the Lompoc plant would make only clear ice. The clear ice of Lompoc would become the source for commercial and residential distribution in the northern county. "At present the [clear] ice used by Lompoc [and Guadalupe] households comes from Santa Barbara."

"Clear ice," Guadalupe plant manager Clint Ferguson explained, "will be made by extracting a large proportion of the air from the water before freezing takes place."[158] This meant that the white ice used for the Lompoc vegetable rail cars would be shipped to Lompoc from the Guadalupe plant.

Fits and Starts

Construction in Lompoc did not go as planned. The new ice plant was once again designed and constructed by Gay Engineering, but steel shipments did not arrive until early January[159] and the massive pair of six-ton diesel compressors did not arrive by rail until February.[160] Opening day came five weeks later than anticipated, and the plant was not making the product it hoped for. Local water was too hard to make clear ice, and a water softener was ordered.

But the news of the day ignored this detail. Clarence Frederick Bacon, assistant manager in Guadalupe, reassigned to oversee the Lompoc plant, gave journalists a tour through the works. "The compressor was started up and workmen were busy mixing the brine for the tank room. Fifteen tons of salt were used to mix the brine and this amount of 'soup' will be sufficient

Aerial view of Puritan Ice, Lompoc, circa 1964. *Lompoc Historical Society.*

to assist in the freezing process for some time...The water for the tanks is secured from a well on the plant property."[161] The first batch of ice was being produced as the local residents read about it in the morning paper.

Not until late in March did Bacon bring the plant to full production, but only temporarily, since the plant was still incapable of producing what Puritan needed to fill its north county clear ice requirements.[162]

Then as the harvest in Guadalupe kicked into high gear in early April, Bacon cranked the plant up to full steam for white ice. He shipped two carloads of ice daily to the Guadalupe plant. Local produce shipments out of Lompoc were also picking up. "The Guadalupe Produce Company [the firm owned and operated by Setsuo Aratani] is shipping a carload of cauliflower every two days, gathering the crop in small lots from various farms. Yesterday the plant began shipping carrots at the rate of two cars a day, the crop coming from the Greco Brothers ranch."[163]

In May, Puritan finally installed the water softener, but before it was in, Lompoc growers swamped the facility with fresh peas, and because Guadalupe and Santa Barbara were both running at capacity, a carload of white ice was also shipped in each day from the Atascadero plant.[164]

Not until July does the harvest taper enough for Bacon to install and perfect the water softening and, subsequently, the manufacture of clear ice to the point of being able to distribute it to local homes and businesses. Asa Williams had the local distributorship agreement with Puritan. The local domestic consumption of ice, previously delivered from Santa Barbara, was averaging six tons per week. "One local bakery is a large user of ice, for it makes its ice cream in its own plant. The ice from the local plant [will be] distributed mostly in Lompoc, Buellton, Solvang and Santa Ynez. [Clear] ice distributed south of Buellton is secured from Santa Barbara."[165]

Lompoc residents continued to receive complete newspaper reports of the plant and of the quantity and value of the produce shipped. In 1937, reporter George Learned delved deeply into the plant and provided a view of the operations:

> *The plant is capable of turning out 300 cakes of ice per day, each weighing 300 pounds* [45 tons]. *Sixty sections comprise the freezing floor with each section made up of six molds. A section weighs nearly half a ton and must be moved with an overhead crane and hoist.* [Sam Hoover, the day engineer], *runs the overhead crane over the desired section and removes the wooden cover unveiling the six connected molds…As he lowers the two hooks and connects onto the section, he starts a motor from the control board on the crane and the section is raised several feet above the floor. It is suspended this way for approximately 20 minutes to let it "sweat"* [by] *leaving the molds hang in normal room temperature until all the frost has melted from the outside and the temperature has raised from three to fifteen* [degrees]. *It is then transported across the room to a concrete trough large enough to submerge the entire section. As it is slowly swung to and fro in water of average temperature, the cakes break loose* [from the ice cans] *and float to the top. From this point the section is set upon a machine that, when the switch is turned on, turns the six molds backwards until they slide down separate chutes and disappear into the storage rooms. Upon pressing another button the machine rights the molds and water is poured into them simultaneously.*[166]

A few months later, in November 1937, Puritan would add a two-hundred-ton storage building to the site in order to meet the continued demand for local ice for vegetable shipments.[167]

During the entire period of the Lompoc plant opening and improvements, Puritan was assisted indirectly but powerfully by a regional booster. Raymond Ellis, a Santa Barbara County farm advisor who led agricultural tours through the area, helped farmers figure out what to plant and market most profitably[168] and wrote articles for the *Los Angeles Times* promoting the area and the best practices for farming here.[169]

When Ellis talked, farmers listened.

"The most important crop to be planted during the spring is lettuce," Ellis wrote, "of which there is slightly over 5,000 acres [in the Santa Maria-Guadalupe-Lompoc valleys]. Most of this crop is planted to come off during the late spring and summer, after the desert deal has been completed. Providing weather conditions are good, a fine quality of summer lettuce is produced in this area, but slime, mildew and tip burn are quite prevalent if the weather isn't just right." The desert deal was the early-to-market harvest that occurred in California's Imperial Valley. According to Ellis, returns in the Lompoc-Guadalupe area on vegetable plantings for 1928 were $2.5 million. For 1929, they were $2 million.[170]

Like Ralph Barrows Easson for the production of poultry in Atascadero, Puritan would hire Ellis in 1931 to run its farming operations in the Guadalupe, Lompoc and Imperial Valleys.

VISTADORES DAYS

The 1930s were good years for the Puritan founders, T.P. Dalzell and L.R. Phillips. Company growth was steady. Their plants in Santa Barbara, Guadalupe, Atascadero and Lompoc provided nearly 100 percent of the ice for Santa Barbara County and a large percentage of the ice for San Luis Obispo County.

While the Depression hit many industries and many families hard, the industrialized model, in large part influenced and created by the railroads, had already displaced millions of farmers into cities, and the cities needed food. Food, especially fresh fruits and vegetables, were increasingly produced in California, and Puritan Ice helped fulfill that demand.

During these years, the two men found time to pursue their private interests. L.R. Phillips purchased the first of several motor yachts and, with his wife, Blanche, and two sons, Donald and Richard, sailed to Europe and the Orient.

T.P. Dalzell purchased the E.W. Ranch, known today as Rancho Oso, on Paradise Road along the Santa Ynez River. He renamed the spread the T.P. Ranch, and he "developed a strain of Morgan horses here that won him many honors." Dalzell also raised cattle on the ranch.[171] He joined the Vistadores, a social ranchers club founded in 1930, and was soon collecting old horse buggies and cars for use in the Vistadores campouts and in the City of Santa Barbara Fiesta parades.

One of these cars came from the original financier of Puritan, Constance Lowell, in 1938. According to Mrs. Lowell's local newspaper, Flagstaff's *Coconino Sun*, "Mrs. Constance E. Lowell yesterday shipped from Lowell Observatory here the 1911 custom-built Stevens-Duryea automobile that she and the late Dr. Percival Lowell once used, to T.P. Dalzell of Santa Barbara, California. Last week Mrs. Lowell shipped two carriages, a phaeton and a runabout, to Mr. Dalzell, who plans to give the three vehicles a comfortable home on his ranch and use them in pageants on the coast."[172]

Regretting the gift of the 1911 Stevens-Duryea some years later, a friend of the Lowells, Dr. Henry Giclas, looked into the whereabouts of what was affectionately known as the "Big Red Car." Dalzell had sold the car sometime in 1946 when he sold the T.P. Ranch. Giclas found an antique dealer who had the car for sale, but he was asking an exorbitant $50,000.

In an interesting aside, in 2002, Mrs. Lowell's great-nephew, William Lowell Putnam, would write an entire book about the car that T.P. Dalzell owned for less than a decade. In *Percival Lowell's Big Red Car*, Putnam relates how, many years later, in 1989, Warwick "Woody" Eastwood acquired a 1911 custom-built red Stevens-Duryea and, while participating in a traveling tour of over one hundred pre-1916 cars, passed through Flagstaff and directly past the Lowell Observatory where Dr. Henry Giclas, now in his eighties, still worked. Giclas saw the car out his office window and commented that the car looked very much like the Big Red Car of Percival Lowell.[173]

On the last day of the tour in Flagstaff, Woody's brother Douglas, who was along for the ride, happened to see the 1915 registration card for the Lowells' 1911 Stevens-Duryea in a display case at the Flagstaff Pioneer Museum. He jotted down the number, 20700, to ask his brother if that car still existed anywhere. Woody's answer was, "Yes, right over there in the parking lot."[174]

In the mid-1990s, Eastwood would sell the car back to the Lowell Observatory at a low price.

SEEDS OF DESTRUCTION

While Puritan's founders enjoyed their rising success through the '30s, the beginnings of the end of the ice dynasty were falling into place.

As with any large shift in history, it is difficult to pinpoint the various causes and how they influenced one another. But one thing is clear: the rail companies' continued allegiance to ice played a significant role in the demise of the railroads as the primary means of transport for perishable goods in the United States.

The railroads had transformed the country in amazing ways. In one blow of the sledgehammer at Promontory Point, Utah, on May 10, 1869, travel from one end of the country to the other had dropped from a grueling three to five weeks to just three days. In the decades after, the railroads had created a distributed food supply network in the United States that increased the variety, freshness and quality of diet for millions of Americans. For the railroads, separating supply from demand by as many miles as possible was a profitable business model, since shippers paid by the mile. The only way to do this successfully for fresh food was by creating a massive network of ice plants across the country.

But the railroads were not fast enough or nimble enough, nor were they far-seeing enough, to address the demands of the many suppliers of perishables in smaller valleys or over more difficult ridges. These farmers were primary movers in applying unified and consistent pressure on the federal government for better roads. The Federal-Aid Highway Act was signed into law by Woodrow Wilson on June 11, 1916, and marked the first time the federal government invested in road building. The program, tellingly managed by the secretary of agriculture, appropriated roughly $5 million the first year and escalated to $75 million by 1922.[175]

As a result of this and subsequent federal acts, the miles of surfaced roads in the United States climbed rapidly and steadily, and many of the vehicles on those new roads were trucks. Rail remains cheaper than truck shipping even today and carries more total freight, but for the lucrative perishable goods business, rail was limited to where the tracks lay, was ponderous in terms of scheduling and demanded economies of scale that left smaller producers without options.

By the 1930s, the truck industry, to address these limitations and to capture an untapped market of small growers, developed mechanical refrigeration. GMC introduced the first refrigerated tractor-trailer in 1931. The U.S. Thermo Control Corporation, which specialized in mechanically refrigerated trailers, was founded in 1941 by Joseph Numero.[176] But the railroads, with their icing infrastructure already in place, were slow to react. The first mechanically refrigerated rail cars did not appear in the rolling stock until 1958.

The stage was set for a swift battle for supremacy in perishable goods, and it would be the demands of a new type of food product that would catapult trucks into the lead.

Birdseye on the Future

Clarence Birdseye, an odd individual with an odd résumé, single-handedly altered the course of human history. According to the Birds Eye corporate website, Clarence, nicknamed "Bugs," earned money for college by trapping and selling black rats to a geneticist at Columbia University and by selling live frogs for use as reptile food to the Bronx Zoo. "His first job after leaving college was as a naturalist with the U.S. Department of Agriculture's Biological Survey, collecting specimens of animals and birds of New Mexico and Arizona. Here he proved himself willing to eat such unusual meats as rattlesnake and is credited with making and eating a soup from mice, chipmunks, gophers, and packrats."[177]

After a stint in Montana studying the Rocky Mountain spotted fever by collecting ticks and their animal hosts, he traveled to Labrador in 1912 to spend the next five years traveling by dog sled to collect fox furs for sale. It was here that "Birdseye tried starlings, blackbirds, whale, porpoise, lynx, alligator, and larger lizards." He was quoted as saying, "I ate about everything...beaver tail, polar bear and [sea]lion tenderloin. And I'll tell you another thing—the front half of a skunk is excellent."[178]

It was in Labrador that Birdseye learned the Eskimos' method of quick-freezing. Done right, the method formed only small ice crystals and retained better flavor and coloring than for fish or meat frozen slowly. Experimenting, Birdseye successfully froze cabbage for later use by his family (he was married in 1915 and brought his wife to Labrador to live) and froze duck and caribou meat under varying conditions.

Distracted by World War I and then by other business pursuits, Birdseye did not focus on frozen foods as an end in themselves again until 1923. When he did, he developed not only a consistent method of fast-freezing

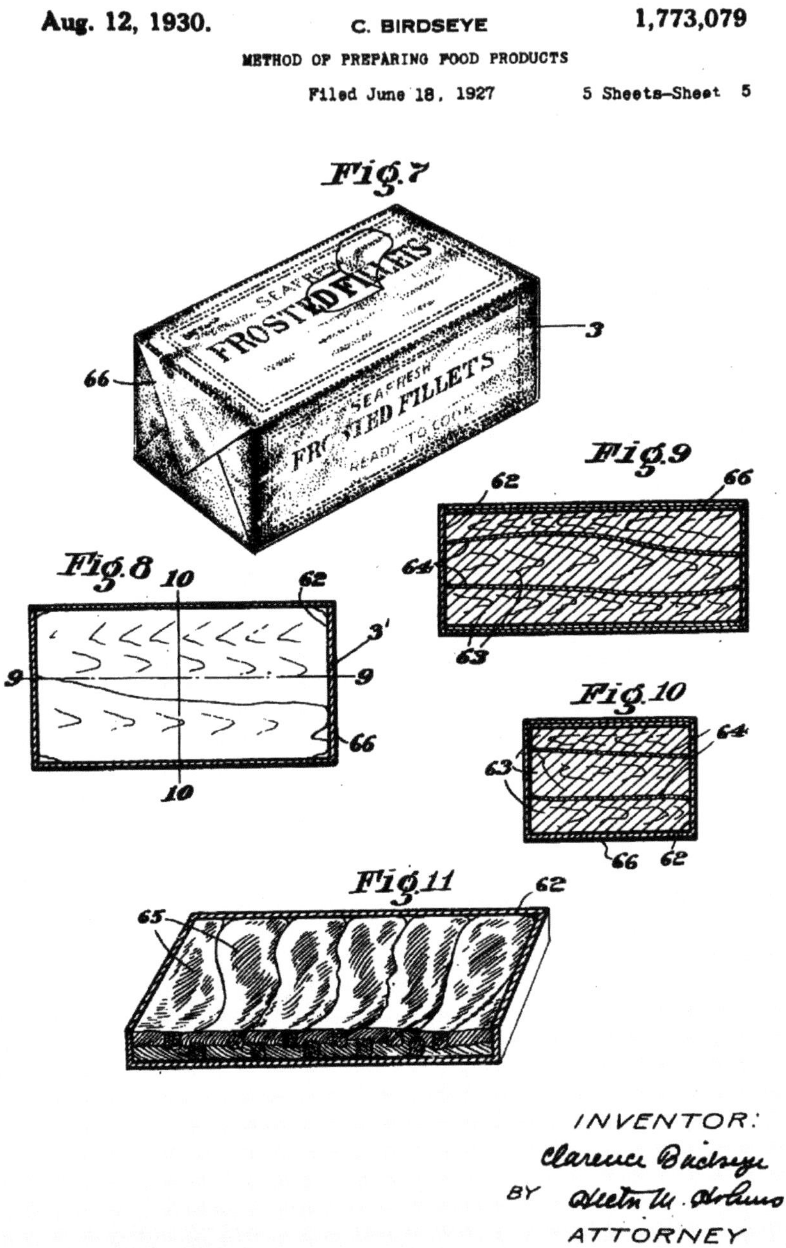

Portion of the Clarence Birdseye patent for packaging frozen fish filets. 1930. *United States Patent Office.*

foods so that they retained their color, flavor and texture but also a means of packaging frozen foods for the end consumer.

In 1929, with all his ducks in a row, he sold his fledgling Birdseye Company to Frosted Foods Company for $22 million. The name was changed to Birds Eye and within a year, on March 6, 1930, twenty-seven vegetables, fruits, fish and meats were test-marketed in eighteen stores in Springfield, Massachusetts.[179]

Over the next decade, as Birds Eye perfected its model and provided the necessary freezers for the stores where its product would be sold, its foods were shipped like any other perishable, in iced rail cars.

But frozen foods needed to be frozen. They could not thaw. The temperatures during transit in rail cars needed to be consistently zero degrees Fahrenheit or lower. The only way to accomplish this was to load massive amounts of salt into the ice bunkers with the ice. Where most fresh produce could ship with minimal or no salt and fresh seafood shipped with an 8 to 10 percent salt solution, frozen foods, whether meats or produce, required as much as 25 percent.

Because of the salt, the rail enterprise was nearly self-corroding. Salt ate away at the steel undercarriage of the refrigerator cars, dripped onto the tracks and shortened the life of the steel rails and, worst of all, ruined hydraulic and electrical equipment for lights, street barricades and switches.

Trucks with mechanical refrigeration units began to appear in large numbers during the late 1930s and 1940s. These offered a consistent zero degrees without salt and without ice, and they could deliver the product to the door of the grocery stores where it was to be sold. Combining this market with the ability to ship produce from off-the-tracks markets, trucking companies delivered a lasting blow to the rail industry.

Lompoc's Meltdown

The Puritan ice plant in Lompoc continued to serve Lompoc and surrounding communities and to ice rail shipments until 1959. Sam Hoover was promoted from day engineer to plant manager when C.F. Bacon retired in the early 1940s.

The Lompoc plant was a terminus, and thus, unlike at Guadalupe and Santa Barbara, the workers at Lompoc did not see the advent of mechanical refrigerator cars. What they did see was the move to trucking.

Because Lompoc agricultural producers were on smaller scale than the cooperatives in Guadalupe and wanted to ship a more varied set of products, it was less cost-effective to use rail. So Puritan followed the market. "Puritan ran a blower for icing trucks," Bill Rule, son of Winifred Rule, former owner of Lompoc Valley Ice Company, recalled. "They'd bring the crops in, put them on conveyors, wash them, box them up, load them on trucks and blow the ice in on top."[180]

But by the late 1950s, more and more trucks were arriving with mechanical refrigeration units, and though they pulled up to the packing sheds on the Puritan site, they bypassed the ice blower.

The Rules' Lompoc Valley Ice Company bought the domestic ice distribution business from Puritan in 1945 and operated it for the last fifteen years of Puritan's time in the valley. Bill Rule recalled traveling out to the Vistadores campouts where T.P. Dalzell—and even possibly L.R. Phillips, who became a member late in the 1930s—may have been encamped:

> *We delivered to every camp, so we got to see what was going on. We met movie stars and celebrities like Joel McCray and Edgar Bergen. I remember The Sons of the Pioneers pulled up in a brand new Buick one year.*
>
> *But* [Puritan] *Lompoc shut down at that point* [1959] *and we started buying from Puritan Santa Barbara. We couldn't buy from Guadalupe because they didn't make clear ice. But, the clear ice in Lompoc* [despite the use of an industrial water softener] *was not as clear as the ice from other places—there were white streaks in our ice here because the water was so hard. Then when Puritan closed the Santa Barbara plant, we bought from Dana Ice, an old family ice company, in San Luis Obispo.*[181]

The Rules dropped the business in the early 1970s as packaged ice and commercial icemakers for restaurants and bars closed out their last markets.

Puritan finally put the property up for sale in 1959. Harold G. Thompson, mayor of Lompoc at the time, contacted old friends and former residents Warren and Violet Bottroff at their home in Oregon and let them know of the property. He also told them, as he looked across the valley toward the rapidly developing Vandenberg Air Force Base, that Lompoc needed a lumberyard. The Bottroffs bought the land, opened a lumberyard as advised and were squarely in line to supply the local construction industry during one of Lompoc's biggest housing booms.[182]

The Bottroffs' purchase was conditional, and for a time, Puritan retained the use of at least some of the site. At some point, Puritan ran a Pepsi distribution dock on the property. Then, in 1971, the Bottroffs paid off the mortgage and acquired adjacent parcels, and Puritan was officially out. One of the old ice storage buildings remains on the site. Louie Dalcerri of Valley Rock Ready-Mix leases a portion of the lot and keeps his office in the old storage building. In the walls is a comfortably insulating 1¾-inch-thick layer of cork.[183]

In 2004, Violet McNett, formerly Violet Bottroff, sold a portion of the site to her son; the remainder she sold to Crown Laurel LLP, a residential homes developer. Model homes went up on the property in 2008, but further site development was halted later that year due to the fall in the housing market.

Chapter 7

Darker Days in Guadalupe

We left Puritan in the midst of its massive expansion of ice making and storage capacity in Guadalupe at the end of Chapter 2. The year was 1926, just three years after the opening of the plant and four years after the founding of the company.

In the coming years, Puritan Ice would be distracted by its battles with Santa Barbara Ice and Ord Ice in Santa Barbara, the sale of Ord Ice to Union Ice in Oxnard, the expansion into Atascadero and the subsequent domination of the national poultry industry and its new ice plant in Lompoc. But through it all, Guadalupe would remain its most productive plant, providing the stability and cash flow the firm needed to launch and manage its other efforts.

But it would not go as the company planned. By 1927, California Lettuce Growers, the firm the Puritan founders had launched to help fill iced rail cars, was shipping…cauliflower.

In fact, along with lettuce, California Lettuce Growers, Inc., was also shipping broccoli, carrots, asparagus and mixed vegetables.

It should not have gone that way. The decade between 1920 and 1930 was the United States' lettuce era. Through the wonders of distributed farming, updated packaging techniques, a national nutritional campaign featuring fresh vegetables and ice, per capita lettuce consumption leaped 300 percent during the decade. The growth curves of the Santa Maria Valley lettuce crop and shipments mirrored those of the Salinas and Imperial Valleys in California and the Salt River basin in Arizona. In fact, Santa Maria's growth

Puritan's California Lettuce Growers started shipping other produce as the lettuce crop weakened in the Santa Maria Valley. Circa 1935. *John Perry collection.*

curve in lettuce production through 1926 perfectly mirrored the Salinas Valley curve—simply a year and few percentage points behind.[184]

Then, in 1927, the *Guadalupe Gazette* reported on the declining quality of lettuce grown on the older fields. Demand for Santa Maria lettuce tapered while the other lettuce-growing regions maintained their high quality and continued to fulfill increased demand. In the Salinas Valley, by 1925, the growth curve was only a quarter of the way up its climb. The Salinas growers would ship 3,581 carloads in 1925. In 1929, the peak of their lettuce years, they would ship 16,312. Puritan, or the Santa Maria Valley, since there was little difference between the two, would ship over 3,000 carloads in 1926 but would drop back below 3,000 in 1927 and remain there the rest of the decade.[185]

With more land and water to throw at the problem, the other valleys simply had more resources. In the Salinas-Watsonville region, over ninety thousand acres were in irrigation. In the Santa Maria Valley, only about twenty-six thousand acres were irrigated. The farming practices used in the Santa Maria Valley could not restore the soil quickly enough to keep growing robust, competitive heads of lettuce.

Some of the Santa Maria Valley harvest left the valley without being tallied. Minami & Sons, known as the lettuce kings of the Santa Maria Valley, would develop a consistent dry-pack lettuce business to Los Angeles over the next few years. It trimmed and packed the lettuce in crates in the early mornings, loaded trucks and drove the produce to the Los Angeles wholesale markets in the cool mornings. This lettuce would not appear on the rail shipment manifests and would not help Puritan meet its icing objectives.

Cold and Calculating

In general, the Japanese grower-shippers were better at soil conservation and maintaining good-quality produce than the other farmers in the Santa Maria Valley, and as a result, their share of the leased farmlands and the shipments grew. In fact, in 1929, California Lettuce formed a coalition of four of the Japanese grower-shipping firms—Guadalupe Produce, Union Produce, Minami & Sons and Santa Maria Produce—and allocated the land California Lettuce controlled among the four. California Lettuce then advertised the valley produce with the four other firms as a single unit.

Starting in 1927, a great deal more land became available in the valley. Union Sugar, which had dominated agriculture in the valley since before the turn of the century, ceased production as sugar markets in Hawaii and Louisiana ate into its market share and prices. When it stopped production, it leased the lion's share of its lands to California Lettuce.

But even the usually effective and persistent Japanese had their problems. During the troubled 1930 season, Japanese lettuce growers in the Guadalupe/Lompoc area lost over $500,000 as the market for vegetables slumped. According to one grower, "carrots had no price, cauliflower was dumped, and lettuce was left unharvested." Ken Kitasako of Tomooka Farms reported that its firm would load rail cars with no destination and start them east as it tried to find a buyer. Many times the company was unable to sell it. The endpoint was Boston. Reminiscent of Steinbeck's six carloads, Kitasako said, "If we got that far, if you didn't sell it, you dump it."[186] Local banks, trusting in their long-term mutually beneficial ties, fronted the Japanese businesses with loans to get them through.

Puritan did not like leaving the company's fate to such vagaries. It wanted to find a way to improve the marketability of the valley's products. It wanted more control. To gain it, the company did what it did best. It put people in charge whom Puritan believed could develop the business strategically. The results were spotty.

Holmes Tabb, the manager of California Lettuce, did not survive with the company through the 1920s. Puritan was soon looking for someone to step in who could do more than make sure everything got shipped on time and at the right temperature. It needed someone who could also strategize, someone who knew what to plant, when, where and why.

The ideal candidate was Santa Barbara County Farm Bureau advisor Raymond Ellis. Ellis traveled the county giving talks about agriculture and publishing pieces on agricultural practices and statistics in the local and regional media.

Filipino or Mexican workers filled the farm labor gap in Guadalupe following the incarceration of the Japanese. *Guadalupe Historical Museum.*

Puritan, as it had done a couple years earlier with Ralph Easson and the poultry farm in Atascadero, hired Raymond Ellis out of a bureaucratic and semi-academic role. His job at Puritan was to establish a research and grower's service department for the Santa Maria Valley and to "study and, if possible, work out a more satisfactory cropping system for the company."[187]

Ellis's stint with California Lettuce was not as clearly documented as was Easson's in Atascadero. Ellis continued to write articles for the local papers and for the *Los Angeles Times*, with the papers remaining vague on the author's affiliation. "Cauliflower," Ellis wrote for the *Times*, "the most important winter crop in the Guadalupe-Santa Maria district, is particularly hard on the soil due to its high water requirements and the harvesting methods used, so it was decided to try cover crops experimentally." The cover crops were grown on Puritan's Betteravia farms. The early results were Whipporwill cowpeas, nine and three-quarter tons per acre, and Virginia soybeans, eleven tons per acre. The planting was done in mid-May, and the crops were turned into the soil in August.[188]

The Virginia soybeans, with their larger tonnage per acre and the production of more nitrogen and other nutrients for the soil, came out ahead.

Little is heard from Ellis after this. His scientific approach would have been painfully slow for Phillips and Dalzell. M.B. "Jack" O'Brien of El Centro was at the helm of California Lettuce shortly after, stepping in from his position as a director of the company to take over the day-to-day management. In 1933, O'Brien, following a more political agenda, got himself appointed the manager of the Santa Barbara County Lettuce Proration Committee.

The committee was formed to create a cooperative among lettuce growers to voluntarily avoid overproduction and depressed prices. By limiting planting acreage (or more often by tilling under portions of a crop) lettuce prices were pushed from .40 cents a crate in June 1933 to $1.25 in October. Though there were Japanese growers on the committee, and cooperation levels were high—they tilled under portions of their fields when asked to—everyone acknowledged that O'Brien pulled the levers.[189]

Another agricultural program developed for California during the Depression was government price supports to put Union Sugar back in operation in 1933. A portion of the acreage in the valley that had been leased to California Lettuce reverted to Union Sugar. But any negative impact on available acreage or the shipments of perishables was easily made up in the large-scale development of new agricultural lands in the valley during the 1930s.

From 1933 through 1937, vegetable acreage in the valley nearly doubled from just over 18,000 acres to over 34,500. The Japanese grower-farmers also liked the new subsidized sugar beet contracts. Many of the growers planted 15 to 20 percent of their total acreage in beets to bolster their incomes.[190]

As in no other region in Southern or Central California, the Japanese thrived in the Santa Maria and Guadalupe Valleys. They proved insightful and nimble in the face of difficulty, and their produce sold faster and for higher prices because they trimmed and packaged it better.

The Sins of the Fathers

By the mid-1930s, however, there were those in the United States who were paying attention to Japan's increasingly militant stance back home.

Aggressions between Japan and China were escalating, and Japan's military spending was rising quickly.

West Coast residents—this was where the Japanese had settled in the United States—were more attuned than others to the perceived threat. In February 1935, Congressman John F. Dockweiler of Los Angeles testified before the House Military Affairs Committee, saying, "I know that 25,000 out of the 100,000 Japanese who are in California are capable of going under arms tomorrow. I am convinced that if we should have any trouble with Japan there would spring up overnight on the Pacific coast an army of 25,000 Japanese reservists."[191]

But Dockweiler's view was not the prevalent one, especially not in the Santa Maria Valley, where the Japanese community was so directly involved in an integrated and successful economic structure.

For one thing, the Japanese in the United States largely saw themselves as Americans. Unlike the Chinese who sent primarily males to work in this country on a long-term but still temporary basis and who in turn sent a substantial portion of their earnings back home, the Japanese brought their families and established stable communities and political ties, essentially making lifetime and multigenerational investments here.

To them, Japan's military machinations seemed distant. Even George Aratani, Setsuo's son, who would take over Guadalupe Produce in 1940 and who in the 1930s was attending Keio University in Japan, remained largely oblivious to Japan's military build-up or its aggressions.[192]

In response to Dockweiler's statements, publicized in the regional papers, Jesse Chambers, secretary of the Santa Maria Chamber of Commerce, wrote to Pat Stubbs, Santa Barbara's congressional representative, "I was very disturbed by Dockweiler's claims which are only his personal opinion…As you know there are a lot of Japanese in this area. I'd like to report that the daily relationship between whites and Japanese are mutually beneficial…They contribute greatly as a group and as individuals to the local community…When there are problems locally, they pitch in to help out." Two Japanese, one of them Setsuo Aratani, served on the board of the local chamber.[193]

Later in 1935, Santa Barbara County supervisor C.L. Preisker boasted that the Japanese in the north county "have become more nearly a part of us than in any other section of the state." They are "highly respected. We have no problem here."[194]

Japan's "Rape of Nanking," a six-week period starting December 13, 1937, was a severe blow to the innocence of the Santa Maria Valley residents,

Japanese and white alike. During the brutal takeover of the Chinese city, the Imperial Japanese Army killed hundreds of thousands of Chinese civilians, disarmed and killed soldiers and raped as many as eighty thousand women.[195]

But while the event received consistent, front-page coverage through the end of 1937 and into the new year, the American media focused mostly on one facet of the battle: the Japanese attack and sinking of the American gunboat *Panay*.[196] Other than this attack in the early hours of the battle, the Japanese command in Shanghai was careful to avoid American and European casualties and thus harsh treatment in the foreign press.

Much of the later coverage of the war in the United States dealt with the strategic efforts of the two armies—attacks made, thrusts thwarted, weather delays—but the horrors of the war filtered through, often in constrained language. "Children and mothers alike were subjected to attacks. Male Chinese civilians who attempted to save their women were shot down in some instances…American and other white women were unmolested."[197]

But as time went on and the savagery went unchecked, journalists tried to express their outrage in print. "The Japanese authorities apologetically admitted to this writer [Hallet Abend] that conditions in Nanking were still deplorable," with troops "out of hand and daily criminally attacking hundreds of women and very young girls." Calling it a "reign of lawlessness and bestiality," Abend stated that major portions of some reports were "actually unprintable."[198]

In a sign of the distance the Japanese in Santa Maria Valley felt from the depredations of their government overseas, George Aratani and other Nisei (American-born Japanese) students remained at Japanese universities, and Issei leaders (first-generation Japanese in America) continued to maintain their bank accounts with Japanese banks.[199]

Not until 1939 would George Aratani return to the United States from Japan, and this was in response to Setsuo Aratani's diagnosis and hospitalization with tuberculosis.

Local Dynasty

By 1940, after three years of continued Japanese aggression overseas, the Japanese in the Santa Maria Valley still held high standing in the community.

Japanese farmers were responsible for the majority of vegetables grown in the Santa Mara and Lompoc Valleys. Their investments of time, finance and wisdom were paying off, and a moderately wealthy class of Japanese was visible in the community. This class was not just the handful of grower-shippers. It extended to business owners along Guadalupe's Main Street, with Japanese-owned restaurants, hotels, garages and other businesses thriving.

When Setsuo Aratani passed away in April of that year, the *Santa Maria Times* ran a front-page eulogy, "Noted Leader of Japanese, Dies." Several days later, an editorial stated, "Setsuo Aratani made a place in the valley that will not soon be filled. That the grief is sincere was fully demonstrated; that his loss will be felt in many quarters is certain."[200]

Aratani's Guadalupe Produce at the time was valued at nearly $2 million. It held over $100,000 in cash and had over $35,000 in receivables. In addition, Aratani held interests in a wholesale produce market in Los Angeles (Los Angeles Vegetable Exchange, founded 1933), a chili-dehydrating plant in Santa Maria (managed by Chester Masunosuke Otoi), a hog farm in Guadalupe, a fertilizer and chemical plant (Guadalupe Fertilizer and Chemical, importing fish meal from Japan) and a small international trading company (All-Star Trading, selling Hiroshima-made sake and fish meal, run by Toshitaro Ishikawa).

Following his father's death, George Aratani, trusting in the network of faithful partners and employees with which Setsuo surrounded himself, returned to Stanford University, where he had been attending since returning to the States.

WINDS OF WAR

As the United States watched war unfold in Europe and the Pacific, discomfort over the Japanese in California increased. In May 1940, Santa Barbara district attorney Percy Heckendorf and several other concerned citizens met with members of the American Legion's Americanization Committee of Santa Maria. The citizens offered their investigative services to identify and stop "fifth-column activities."[201] Fifth-column was a term coined by Emilio Mola, a Nationalist general during the 1936–39 Spanish Civil War who stated during an attack of Madrid that the four columns

Anti-Japanese cartoon, one of many, drawn by Dr. Seuss during World War II. The fifth column was a feared organization of militant Japanese civilians in the United States. 1942. *PM Magazine.*

of his forces outside the city would be supported by a "fifth column" of supporters inside the city.

Though not directly intended to address Japanese in this country—the law was originally proposed by Howard W. Smith to persecute socialists who were organizing and inciting unions in the East and Midwest—the federal Alien Registration Act of 1940 made the "intent to cause the overthrow or destruction" of any government endeavor a criminal act. However, it also stated, "A fine of $1,000 or imprisonment for six months, or both, is the penalty for any alien who fails to register and submit to fingerprinting, or for failure of a guardian to register an alien minor under 14 years of age." This portion of the law, since most immigrants to the United States were not considered aliens, was directed for the most part at the Asian population in the country. Passed in August 1940, the law gave aliens such as the Issei (first-generation Japanese-Americans) in Santa Maria Valley, until the twenty-sixth of December to report to the local post office.[202]

On October 17, the federal draft board announced that all Nisei (second-generation Japanese Americans) males between the ages of eighteen and thirty-five must register for the draft.

Soon after this sudden shift in federal focus, the Issei and Nisei grower-shippers associated with Guadalupe Produce met with Leo T. McMahon, the legal counsel for Puritan Ice Company and California Lettuce. On November 8, 1940, in order to protect the assets of the Issei founders, they formed a holding company, Vegetable Farms, Inc., owned by three Nisei: George Aratani, Butch Tamura and Miyokichi Matsuno.[203] Nisei could still legally own land and businesses.

The Issei, as directed, reported to the local post office. The Nisei, as directed, registered for the draft. At the Santa Barbara County Fair in July 1941, the Japanese growers in the north county created a weeklong extravaganza and won many of the produce and packaging awards. The *Santa Maria Times* was impressed.

But a few short months later, on December 7, 1941, the Japanese bombed Pearl Harbor, triggering the United States' entry into World War II and a drastic and permanent change to farming on the Central Coast.

TICKLISH TASK

Within hours of the attack, the FBI picked up fourteen Issei and one Nisei, Butch Tamura of Guadalupe Produce, in the Santa Maria Valley. Across the country, 734 Issei were incarcerated, and all Issei assets were frozen across the board.

In Santa Maria, the *Times* editor, G.A. Martin, called the task before the local population "ticklish." Is it, Martin asked in an editorial, "fair to ourselves or to our nation to continue to accept all [the local Japanese] in the same unquestioning manner in which they have been accepted in the past? It is not our fault if the race to which they belong has…demonstrated that to trust it is to be deceived."[204]

European and American growers and shippers in other valleys, especially in the Salinas area, found nothing ticklish about it. They came

A California Vegetable Growers label from the Guadalupe region. 1943. *John Perry collection.*

out immediately for a complete and unprecedented evacuation of not just the Issei, but of their sons and daughters, the Nisei, who had been born in the United States and who were therefore by law U.S. citizens.

Aratani and the other Nisei again met with McMahon on December 14, this time transferring all the assets of the incarcerated Issei founders, and their own, into Vegetable Farms, Inc., for protection. George Aratani was appointed general manager of the corporation, effective December 7, 1941, "with full power and authority to act for the corporation in all situations and in every transaction."[205]

A few days later, it was discovered that the California State license for the chili dehydrating plant that Aratani now co-owned had lapsed. Chili stood bright in the fields ready for harvest. It would wilt and lose its value in a matter of days. The other owner, Otoi, was Issei and incarcerated, so the state would not renew the license. Aratani, attempting to preserve the value in the business for both himself and for Otoi, petitioned the California State Agricultural Department and traveled to Los Angeles for a hearing on the license, but to no avail. The only avenue available to Aratani was to purchase Otoi's share of business, or sell the business outright, in order to remove the Issei shadow from the title.[206]

This case exemplifies numerous instances where the Nisei leadership in the Santa Maria and Lompoc Valleys scrambled to identify and recast ownership to protect the value of the assets of the Issei.

Meanwhile, the demand to extend the arrests to all people of Japanese descent in this country heightened. S.V. Christierson, president of the Western Growers' Protection Association (WGPA) and E.M. Seifert, a director of the WGPA and president of the Salinas Grower Shipper Vegetable Association, launched an aggressive anti-Japanese letter-writing campaign to California authorities and congressmen. They wrote to Earl Warren, then the State of California attorney general, stating, "We must eliminate as many of these undesirable aliens from the lands of California as is possible." They cited the Santa Maria Valley Japanese, with their stronghold on agriculture in the region, as evidence that the Japanese would soon take over California agriculture.[207]

In California, Earl Warren spearheaded the movement to remove all Japanese, both Issei and Nisei, from their homes and intern them at relocation camps for the duration of the war. Santa Barbara district attorney Percy Heckendorf pressed for the same from within the county.

The Nisei met once again with Leo McMahon, this time to discuss what could be done to protect Nisei assets should the campaigns be successful. McMahon recommended a holding company managed by Puritan Ice as being the best method available. Given their limited options, it made sense. According to Kent Haldan, who completed a dissertation on the Santa Barbara County Japanese populations for the years 1900 to 1960, "The Puritan Ice Company and its subsidiary the California Lettuce Growers opposed the evacuation movement. Leo McMahon, vice president and legal counsel for Puritan Ice, met with Chet Moore and other officials of the WGPA and expressed his opposition to their evacuation movement." In addition, Jack O'Brien of California Lettuce "was an outspoken defender of the Santa Maria Japanese [and was] extremely unpopular" with the white grower-shippers throughout California because of this.[208]

On February 18, 1942, a major sweep completed the FBI roundup of Issei. The next day, President Franklin Delano Roosevelt signed into law Executive

Order 9066 empowering the United States Army to designate military areas from which "any or all persons may be excluded" and transported elsewhere. The law was immediately applied to the Nisei of California.[209]

Freezing Point

In Los Angeles County, the response was to set up a governmental committee that would oversee the Japanese leases. Perhaps to avoid being subjected to the whims of a committee, Puritan founders Phillips and Dalzell created California Vegetable Growers, Inc., a holding company that paralleled the role of their firm California Lettuce Growers but which would fulfill those functions on the Japanese-held assets. Leo McMahon met with the Nisei representatives of the Japanese firms in February and March and proposed that they place their firms into California Vegetable to protect their assets.

According to McMahon, the firm was created as a trust to "operate the growing, packing, and shipping operations of the three farmers while the managers were in confinement." When the war was over, "the trust would be dissolved and the individual companies would revert to their original management." It was the only option available to the farmers to retain any assets at all should the Nisei lose their rights as citizens. For Puritan, the deal ensured that a crucial source of supply would not be interrupted or lost. Details were not worked out, but Puritan promised to provide regular operating reports and accounts, and a cursory but broadly scoped agreement was signed.[210]

At the point when the firm's assets were transferred into the trust, Minami and Guadalupe Produce were both valued at over $2 million and had cash assets of $250,000 and $114,000 respectively. Both firms also owned some land outright. The smaller Tomooka Farms was valued at $500,000.

On April 25, nearly one thousand Japanese Nisei from the Santa Maria Valley, among them the Nisei owners of the firms under the new California Vegetable umbrella, climbed aboard buses and traveled to a hastily erected relocation center near Tulare, California.

Almost immediately, the Japanese had misgivings. Something had shifted. Puritan did not, in fact, provide reports. Instead, through letters from Puritan's secretary-treasurer Paul Danielson, and during a visit to

American Japanese gathering at Christ United Methodist Church in Santa Maria, preparing for internment at the Tulare Assembly Center. April 30, 1942. *Black Gold Cooperative Library System.*

the camp from California Lettuce Growers manager Joe Kantor, the company complained of the difficulties it was having. Field laborers, it said, many of them Filipino, their homeland under attack from Japanese forces, refused to work for California Vegetable Growers because of the Japanese ownership.

George Aratani and other Nisei principals wrote to company employees still working at the farm sheds to verify the reports. Their employees wrote back, "No problems that we can see."[211] But there was nothing the Nisei could do from their cots in a fenced encampment 160 miles to the north.

The Japanese owners' frustration increased as they attempted to address the business issues they confronted—not just seized assets but also active debts, tax problems, homes and businesses left empty and the confusing reports of the Puritan officials—from imprisonment.

In September 1942, McMahon called together the Nisei principals of the three firms at the Gila River relocation center—they were permitted to travel between camps for such purposes—and told them, "We're getting to a point where we can't operate very well with a trust" due to the labor problems. He proposed that Puritan would buy their operations outright.[212]

Puritan Ice ad, stating, "A true American citizen—entitled to boast that honor—must be an American citizen not alone by accident of birth or privilege of naturalization." In an oblique way, this rules out the Nisei. 1944. *Santa Barbara Public Library.*

Without complete information and their backs once again against the wall, Guadalupe Produce and Tomooka Farms both reluctantly agreed to the deal. Minami refused, preferring to keep the trust functioning.

The purchase price for the $2 million Guadalupe Produce, even as vegetable prices and the value of every asset the company owned was climbing through the roof due to the war, was $250,000. For the half-million-dollar Tomooka Farms assets, the purchase price was $75,000.

Minami ended up selling a year later after attempting legal action against Puritan. With Puritan running the firm and the Minamis in relocation camps, Puritan held all the cards. But even so, Puritan's dealings were called "dirty" by impartial attorneys. The sticking point was $12,000 of equipment Puritan acquired in the initial trust agreement with Minami. The Minami Company wanted this equipment returned to them. Puritan agreed but used a current valuation, meaning that a 1942 fleet of tractors, trucks, trailers and other equipment became no more than a couple trucks and tractors in 1943.

James Terry, the Gila River attorney, stated that Puritan's position was "as damaging to our relations with this minority as is the unjust vituperation and propaganda spreading and increasing throughout" California. In response to the Minami's legal action against them to restore the $12,000 of equipment, Puritan sued the Minamis for libel and "malicious prosecution."[213]

Not everyone on the Puritan team felt the same way. According to John McReynolds—whose recent book, *Vanished, Lompoc's Japanese: Of One Hundred Families Only Two Returned*, delves into the history of the Japanese in Lompoc—both Jack O'Brien and a man named William Fisk were fired by Puritan because they disagreed with the plan to buy out the trusts.[214]

Nothing Is the Same

When Puritan took over the $300,000-plus cash assets of Guadalupe Produce and Minami and Sons, it quickly spent it in Blythe, where it had built its latest ice plant. It went to buy much-needed vegetable and melon farmland in a highly competitive new market.

The sudden field labor problem in California, caused by the incarceration of the Japanese farmers, was solved through the duration of the war by the first concentrated national campaign, the Bracero Program, to import seasonal Mexican laborers. White growers stepped into the ownership and management roles left vacant by the relocated and decapitalized Japanese.

During negotiations for bringing in Mexican nationals to harvest and pack vegetables in California, Puritan encountered the gregarious secretary-treasurer of the local Teamsters Union, H. Don Underwood. In 1943, Underwood would come work for Puritan Ice. In a few years, rising quickly through the organization, Underwood would become the company's CEO and take the firm in new and profitable directions. For now, he would manage the large personnel force of field laborers, packers and office staff for California Lettuce and California Vegetable in Lompoc and Guadalupe.

Frozen Assets

As the war came to a close and the Japanese were released from the relocation centers across the West, those whose properties were still in trust or under lease returned to the Guadalupe area, hoping to pick up somewhere close to where they left off.

However, one example of their reception will stand for many others. Students returning to Santa Maria High School were shunned, and the occasional rock was thrown. The Future Farmers of America distributed pins at the school depicting a coiled snake with a Japanese face. It read, "MY PLEDGE—IN MEMORY of the victims of PEARL HARBOR, BATAAN, CORREGIDOR and ALL OTHER JAPANESE ATROCITIES and, because there is no proof of Japanese loyalty to my government, ON MY HONOR AS AN AMERICAN I pledge not to TALK TO, PATRONIZE, ASSOCIATE, or FRATERNALIZE WITH ANY JAPANESE."[215]

Puritan, for its part, was well over any notions of paternalism, fairness or even legality where the Japanese were concerned.

One lease Puritan held in trust and refused to relinquish after the war ended up in the County Superior Court and set legal precedence for numerous cases in California in the coming months. The lease was for Harold Shimizu's Grower's Garage, a "large and highly integrated automobile sales and maintenance operation—which included a Chevrolet dealership, an engine repair shop, an auto body shop, and a glass shop." California Lettuce

Harold Shimizu's garage, later renamed Grower's Garage. 1936. *Black Gold Cooperative Library System.*

brought suit against Shimizu, claiming it was entitled to hold the property until Japan signed a treaty with the United States.[216]

Santa Barbara Superior Court judge Louis Drapeau ruled against California Lettuce and in favor of Shimizu. Puritan had leased Shimizu's garage for the "duration of the present war." Drapeau stated that since the lease was for an uncertain time period, it was effectively a month-to-month lease, and seeing that the Japanese had surrendered, California Lettuce must release the property immediately.[217]

Other Japanese businessmen in the region also had trouble with Puritan. Bill Kashigawa, who leased his family hotel to Puritan, had to hire a lawyer and had a hard time getting it back.

News of the poor reception in Guadalupe filtered back to the relocation centers, and families who were still finding out where their friends and family were planning to go and organizing themselves to move made other choices.

Frozen Out

Maybe Puritan had it coming, but with its focus shifting to Blythe and a shift among the powers that be in the agricultural world of the Santa Maria Valley, Puritan was essentially frozen out of its home turf of Guadalupe over the next five years. Three factors came into play.

The first was a souring of its relationship with Union Sugar. In 1927, when Union had shut down its Betteravia operations just down the rail line from Puritan's Guadalupe ice plant, Puritan had been a beneficiary of hundreds of acres of productive farmland suddenly turned to use as vegetable fields. Then, in 1933, when Union resurrected its plant at Betteravia, Puritan's tight-knit group of growers benefited as government price supports for sugar beets provided a stable income source while the company rapidly expanded to new acreage.

California Lettuce, in taking over the acreage previously farmed by the Japanese, also took over the sugar beet agreements. From 1942 through 1949, California Lettuce continued to work out new contracts with Union Sugar for the growing and delivery of beets. The terms of the agreements and the acreage changed over the years, but in 1949, under an agreement to grow 239 acres of beets, California Lettuce grew and delivered only 117 acres of beets.

Japanese workers harvesting sugar beets in Guadalupe. 1936. *Black Gold Cooperative Library System.*

What ensued was four years of legal battles in the California Supreme Court on the nature of contract law. In the end, on October 19, 1953, the court finally found in California Lettuce's favor for a sum of $32,710.83, nearly $280 an acre of delivered beets. But by then, California Lettuce was no longer doing business in the Santa Maria or Lompoc Valleys.[218]

Obviously, 239 acres one way or another was not going to make or break California Lettuce. But the legal suit references "charges for the use of other acreage," and this was one place where Union Sugar could hurt California Lettuce financially by leasing its land to a direct Puritan competitor.

WEST VERSUS EAST, ON A SMALL SCALE

When Puritan arrived in Guadalupe, there was one other farming and ice concern immediately to the east. Captain G. Allan Hancock, who became Santa Maria's leading developer and financier, had already made the family fortune as a young man. His family owned what became the La Brea Tar Pits in Los Angeles, where a wealth of oil had been pumped out of the ground before the family donated the land to the City of Los Angeles.

"Retiring" at the age of forty-five to Santa Maria in 1920, Hancock created a small business fiefdom that consisted of an integrated farming operation, an ice and cold storage plant and the Santa Maria Valley Railroad. The farming operation, Rosemary Farm, became and remains well known for its poultry and eggs. The railroad carried freight and passengers, but the bulk of its workload was the transport of feed to his poultry farms and the transport of iced eggs and fresh produce to rail sidings at Guadalupe.[219]

In the late 1940s and the early 1950s, as relations with California Lettuce soured and its land leases came up for renewal, Union Sugar simply leased the land it had previously leased to California Lettuce to Rosemary Farm. These two factors—the loss of Union Sugar land and goodwill, and Rosemary Farm stepping in to take over the land—sent California Lettuce out of the valley for good. Its headquarters would remain in Santa Barbara, but its primary operations would shift to Blythe, California.

The last factor in Puritan's overall demise in the Santa Maria Valley was the dwindling of demand for ice. The peak year for perishables by rail in the United States was 1946. That year, Pacific Fruit Express shipped more than 465,000 carloads of perishables. By 1954, the total had dropped below 400,000 cars.[220]

The reasons were the rise in demand for frozen foods, which could not ship effectively by rail because of the extreme requirement for salt, and the parallel rise in the number of mechanical refrigeration units on trucks to supply that demand. Since Los Angeles and San Diego were viable markets for truck-shipped produce, Santa Maria and Lompoc Valley growers began to shift some of their perishables to trucks.

But Puritan still believed in the ice business. The plants in Guadalupe, Lompoc and Santa Barbara remained open to ice and re-ice the rail cars, whether they originated from San Francisco or from farms in the Santa Maria Valley. In Guadalupe, the plant increasingly shipped ice across its lot to the packing sheds, where big ice shredders ran through the days and nights at harvest time, and the ice went out by rail or truck.

To try to place the firm back in the forefront of the perishables cooling industry in the valley, Puritan built a vacuum pre-cooling facility in Guadalupe in 1952. Industry forefront or not, it was an acknowledgement of defeat. Pre-cooling methods were in place as early as 1909, when the practice of chilling citrus fruits prior to shipment in California towns like Colton and Roseville "d[id] away almost entirely with the use of ice in the shipment of fruit," leading one ice plant operator to claim a bit prematurely, "This [ice] business has all gone to smash."[221]

The vacuum plant at Guadalupe used newer, vastly improved technology, but it, too, significantly reduced the need for ice.

The vacuum pre-cooling apparatus consisted of four packing lines that extended by conveyor into semi-truck-sized cylindrical steel chambers. When a full conveyor of produce in its waxed and water-resistant packaging was queued inside the chamber, the vegetables were sprayed with a mist of cold water. The conveyor lines could then be "cut" and two steel doors closed on either end of the chamber. Very quickly, a vacuum was created, drawing temperatures from as high as ninety degrees Fahrenheit down to thirty-six degrees, or nearly freezing. The process required between thirty and forty minutes as the temperature of the inner layers of the produce radiated outward and cooled to a more moderate forty to fifty degrees.

Then the steel doors were opened, the conveyor tracks reconnected and the produce pushed into an insulated truck or rail car. Chilled at the outer layers, the produce continued to cool over the next hour or so. If the distance the produce traveled was far, ice was also shredded and blown over the crates. But with chilled produce, the ice had less work to do and lasted longer.

Building the first Puritan pre-cooling plant at Guadalupe in 1952. *Rennie Pili collection.*

Puritan's pre-cooling plant as it appeared in 1984. *Bruce Phillips collection.*

The Guadalupe facilities—the ice plant, the farming relationships and the new pre-cooling plant—were overseen by Clinton B. Ferguson, a man who had rowed crew with Leon Phillips at Cornell and who had been with the firm since the early days. Richard Phillips, the eldest of Leon's two sons, who had started with the firm in Blythe in 1950, moved to the Santa Maria Valley in 1952 to manage the pre-cooling plant. Richard would remain as general manager following Ferguson's retirement in the late 1950s.[222]

The Puritan plant in Guadalupe continued making ice even as, in 1971, Pacific Fruit Express, its primary buyer in the early days, placed its last order. In 1986, with the ice plant and the pre-cooling plant still in fitful operation, Puritan Ice was sold to James Lindsey of Bakersfield. He was, according to one source central to the Puritan story, no more than a front man for a very large corporation. More on this in the closing chapters.

In 1998, with the plant still functioning, partners Rennie Pili and Thomas Chan purchased the plant from Lindsey. They ran it with no substantial modifications until 2008, when the demand for ice for perishables in Guadalupe finally evaporated.

It was what happened in Blythe that set the stage for the end of Puritan Ice.

Chapter 8

Ice in the Desert

Puritan founders Leon Phillips and T.P. Dalzell had somehow known a market for lettuce grown south of Salinas would spring up in the early 1920s before anyone else in the ice business. It happened again, in 1941, when Puritan appeared in Blythe, California, and incorporated a new ice company the day after the Japanese attack on Pearl Harbor.

California's Imperial Valley, ninety miles northeast of Blythe, was already an ice kingdom to make any iceman salivate. The heat and rich soil, combined with irrigation, fostered a robust and nearly yearlong profusion of vegetables and melons. To get this bounty to tables in the East, a great deal of ice was needed. Puritan, with its Atascadero poultry farm coming to an end and the produce business in Guadalupe getting squeezed by Salinas and Imperial Valley products, wanted a piece of the desert market. The Palo Verde Valley, spreading out from Blythe, California, was just the place.

In Santa Barbara County, the knowledge of the impending 1923 Santa Margarita Agreement most likely came through Phillips's and Dalzell's employment at the Los Angeles–based refrigeration engineering firm, Gay Engineering. In Blythe, the knowledge seems to have come through contacts at Pacific Fruit Express and possibly at Santa Fe Railroad.

For whatever reason, it appears from the evidence that Phillips and Dalzell were aware, before the United States declared war in either the Pacific or European theaters, that the country would go to war and that a military desert training center with the express purpose of preparing troops for battle in North Africa would be developed near Blythe.

That training center would, of course, require ice.

BLYTHE, IN SHORTHAND

Like the Imperial Valley, Blythe is a hot spot. For nearly half the year, the average temperature is ninety degrees or higher. Like most desert regions, the place can also get cold, dipping below freezing on an average of twenty days a year. Precipitation runs a thirsty four inches a year. Underfoot, the land is a large alluvial plain deposited over the millennia by the Colorado River.

If you can get water, the place is ideal for vegetables and melons.

Appropriately enough, the town is named for the man who first acquired water rights in the area. Thomas Blythe, wealthy from real estate investments in San Francisco, acquired the water rights in 1877. In 1882, with partners William Calloway and George Irish, he attempted to farm in the area. But Blythe died a year later, and no real development occurred until after the turn of the century.[223]

The first successful enterprise in the valley was a cattle spread started in 1904 and run by Arizonans Frank Murphy and Ed Williams. With W.A. Hobson, they formed the Palo Verde Land and Water Company. W.F. Holt, who later helped develop the Imperial Valley into a farming mecca, was the company's general manager.

But Blythe was a remote outpost until August 8, 1916, when the California Southern Railroad built a spur line to the town. In anticipation of this great event, the town incorporated in July of that year.

Then, in 1919, E.S. Kassler, who owned several ice plants in the Imperial Valley, crossed the ridge and built Blythe's first ice and cold storage plant, the Imperial Ice Company. For the first time, local farms could ice and ship their perishables to markets outside the region, but the main users of the ice were the local residents and businesses. They needed it.

PALO VERDE PERISHABLES

Having ice and rail was not enough to put the Palo Verde Valley on the fruits and vegetables map. Even the installation of a second ice plant by the Palo Verde Creamery in 1922 did not create the rapid spread of agriculture in the area that was seen elsewhere. Palo Verde Creamery bought out Imperial Valley Ice to become the sole ice producer in town in 1934, but rail ice remained a minor source of business.

Then, a year later, in 1935, Eaton Brothers, a family farming business, built a packing shed to the south of town and began growing, packing and shipping lettuce, carrots, broccoli and cantaloupes. Still, the volume did not approach that of other similar regions. By 1941, Eaton was shipping just 106 carloads of winter vegetables—lettuce and carrots—using Palo Verde Creamery ice.

Nevertheless, Eaton and Palo Verde Creamery saw themselves as the local monopoly. Other growers built packing sheds alongside the Eaton Brothers' sheds in the late 1930s, but their volume was even less. There was really no one else in town that could control the growing or icing ends of the business.

Then, on December 8, 1941, while the news headlines were filled with the bombing of Pearl Harbor the day before, Phillips and Dalzell quietly incorporated a company they called Blythe Ice. The town would not learn of the new kids in town until January 22, 1942, when the *Palo Verde Times* would announce on the front page, "Blythe Ice Co to Build Ice Plant South of Town."[224]

Planning for War

The incorporation of Blythe Ice was yet another point of departure for the Puritan Ice directors. Names in addition to L.R. Phillips and T.P. Dalzell had appeared on incorporation papers for California Lettuce Growers, Puritan Poultry and California Vegetable Growers, but Blythe Ice, coming as it did twenty years after the founding of the company, was the first time one of the sons of the founders appeared as an officer. Donald Dalzell, at this point thirty-two years of age, was named president of Blythe Ice.

This was the moment in the company's history when the notion of turning the reins over to the sons was experimented with. Donald was the first to be given a substantive title and responsibility. Later, the Phillips' sons, Richard and Don, would also be given the opportunity. Ultimately, the experiment failed on all counts. The Donald Dalzell experiment was short-lived.

Donald Dalzell was the first experiment in keeping it in the family because he was twelve years older than the eldest Phillips son, Richard. He had, by all accounts, a reckless youth. In 1926, Puritan bookkeeper Harry Nethery, aged thirty, was killed in an automobile accident at Garden and Arrellaga in

Donald Dalzell at the Blythe Ice plant, 1942. *Connie Phillips collection.*

Santa Barbara. The car flipped at good speed. Donald Dalzell, aged sixteen, was driving.[225]

There were two sides to the story of why Donald Dalzell was made president of Blythe Ice. One side stated that Donald was being kicked upstairs to get him out of headquarters, still located in the utilitarian ice plant at 325 East Cabrillo Boulevard in Santa Barbara. The other side said that Donald was the one who brokered the Blythe desert ice deal for the company.

According to most accounts, though, Donald did not move to Blythe to take command until construction was well underway in March. It was T.P. who came down and got the first Blythe dust on his shoes. In a January 22, 1942 *Palo Verde Times* piece, T.P. is quoted as saying, "The plant will supply the requirements of the Santa Fe railroad and growers and shippers of perishable commodities produced in and shipped from Palo Verde Valley." In conjunction, "a highly developed shipping center of approximately 15 acres for the location and building of packing houses and general shipping facilities will be provided."[226]

The plant is wrapped in mystery. The *Palo Verde Times* continued to report progress on the plant as though it were being built from the ground up like the company's plants in Santa Barbara, Guadalupe and Lompoc. But former employees Sidney Grande and Pete Compten both recalled that the plant was dismantled elsewhere and shipped to Blythe. The origin of the

The Phillips brothers, Donald and Richard, with their Lincolns. Circa 1950. *Bruce Phillips collection.*

plant remains unknown. "It was a plant they bought out up in Guadalupe. It came in on rail cars and they put it back together."[227]

Given the ramp up of most manufacturing and fabrication plants for the war effort, the strategy makes sense. However, no evidence of another plant in the Guadalupe area, or of any sizable purchase of any plant by Puritan, has surfaced in the available records.

The new-used ice plant was to have a one-hundred-ton-per-day manufacturing capacity, with two thousand tons of storage. Target completion was late May 1942. Donald Dalzell arrived on site that same month and took charge.[228]

A Grande Move

In April 1942, packing sheds were going up and the firm was predicting that it would be in line for the upcoming cantaloupe harvest that would start in

Sydney Grande on the ice platform in Blythe, 1943. *Blanche Copeland collection.*

June. But on June 11, when the packing of melons started, the packing went through the Palo Verde Ice Company. There were 940 acres of cantaloupes with roughly 100 crates per acre shipped. Blythe Ice was not yet ready to provide ice.

That same day, the local paper reported that Blythe Ice would freeze its first fifty tons over the weekend, but full capacity was two weeks out. The plant promised both white and clear ice.[229]

But contracts for cantaloupes did not materialize. Neither did the promised Desert Training Center and its supposed demand for ice appear. Burning through the wages of a forty-five-man construction crew and struggling to obtain materials, Puritan sidelined Donald Dalzell to more of a figurehead manager and reassigned the lead engineer from the Santa Barbara plant, Sidney Grande, to finish building the Blythe Ice plant. When the plant opened, Puritan management asked him to stay, leaving Donald Dalzell sidelined more or less permanently.

Sidney Grande was to remain in Blythe the rest of his life, and he and his family left a permanent imprint on the area. People in Blythe remember the Grandes today. Sidney Grande ran the plant from 1942 until he retired in 1966. There were several children, and son John ran the plant from 1966 until the plant was finally sold in 1975. Blanche Copeland, daughter of Sidney, still lives across the river in Parker, Arizona, and provided excerpts from notes Sidney Grande wrote about their early years in town:

> *We had 1 day a week off, usually a weekday. I stayed with* [Puritan] *through the years and in 1942 they sent me to Blythe, where they were building a string of packing sheds and they had bought an old ice plant and moved it to Blythe. I was supposed to stay there long enough to help set the machines up and then go back to Santa Barbara, but in 3 months they had me go back and move the family down. We rented our house* [on Milpas Street in Santa Barbara] *and loaded everything on trucks to haul to Blythe. We were supposed to have a house to live in but we had to live in one big room they had until the people moved out of the house on the ranch.*
>
> *When we got the plant running we had to ship all the ice we made to the army and the air base on the mesa. This was where the B-17s were and later the B-24s. This was the last training place for them before they went overseas. General Patton used the room we had used when we first came to Blythe as his command post and office. In later years they increased the capacity of the plant to 200 tons more a day, which we were still shipping to the army and using some in the packing sheds.*[230]

When the plant finally opened in early July 1942, it was to a muted demand for ice. Local growers remained mostly loyal to Palo Verde Ice, and word had not yet come on the military training center. Desperate to get the ice business in Blythe launched, Puritan took the cash from the Guadalupe Produce deal and took out an additional $50,000 loan from the County Bank in Santa Barbara.[231] With the money, California Lettuce Growers, once again creating its own market for ice, became the largest grower in the Palo Verde Valley overnight. Calling them the "valley's biggest vegetable grower," the paper stated that in early October 1942, "Palo Verde Valley's newest vegetable shipper, the California Lettuce Growers, will have some 1,000 acres in lettuce and carrots here."[232]

A month later, with a U.S. Army brigadier general named George Patton staying at one of the residences on the grounds of Blythe Ice, the approval of the Desert Training Center was finally announced. Patton and his staff would soon be training over one million troops in camps scattered over the region, all of them needing ice for food preservation, cooling systems and medical purposes.

Blythe Ice had a market.

Production Runs

By 1943, California Lettuce Growers and Blythe Ice had hit their stride. The plant was shipping winter vegetables in January with thirty truckloads and three rail cars of carrots to Los Angeles in a single month. The company also introduced cauliflower to the valley, shipping 142 crates the first year.[233] A week later, with a cold snap ruining a week of lettuce harvests in the Imperial Valley and sending prices up, California Lettuce trucked 14,000 crates of lettuce, mostly to Los Angeles and mostly dry-pack (without ice).[234]

In February, another new grower appeared in the valley, with yet another innocuous name: California Produce. It announced the planting of six hundred acres of cantaloupes for the 1943 season and set about building a shed on Blythe Ice land.[235] Later on, California Produce would intermingle its business more closely with Puritan, as though it may have been acquired by Puritan, but the ownership remains cloudy in today's records.

Building on lessons learned from the Japanese, California Lettuce shipped celery in from Guadalupe and repackaged it in order to build out cars of mixed vegetables and fulfill orders to the military camps. In April, it introduced sweet corn and started planting for the cantaloupe season.[236]

But the news was not all about California Lettuce and Blythe Ice. Eaton Brothers' and other local growers' shipments received coverage in the same news articles, and their share of the market, while never quite as much as California Lettuce, slowly increased. In early February, Eaton moved thirty-five cars of carrots and thirty-five of lettuce, just as California Lettuce's shipments were tapering off. Through June and July, Eaton and Comer, another local grower, maintained a larger number of shipments than in previous years.[237]

Then, on July 29, just as "the Cantaloupe Deal," as the papers called it, was completed, a lightning strike burned the Eaton Brothers packing shed and offices to the ground. Lost in the blaze were a large concrete basement,

Early photo of Blythe Ice, 1942. *Connie Phillips collection.*

offices, heavy-duty ramps, all their loading conveyors and a few thousands dollars of inventory.[238]

By now, Puritan had completed the takeover of Minami Farms in Guadalupe and Lompoc and the $225,000 cash in its safe. Puritan, operating under the name of California Vegetable Growers for the first time in the Blythe region, now used that money to drastically extend its agricultural landholdings in the valley. It presented the Palo Verde Irrigation District with plans to develop "several thousand acres of new land, much of it outside the Colorado River levee."[239]

Eaton rebuilt its operation, and the vegetable race in the valley continued.

The Southern California Market

With naval and military bases and hundreds of defense factories clustering in Southern California during the war, vegetable and fruit growers saw their market shifting from the east to the much more accessible market of Southern California. "Growers figure that with the big increase in Southern California population and with Japanese growers not active this year, most of the crop can be marketed in the southland."[240]

The prediction, made in April 1943, would turn out to be true. By year's end, "practically all the shipments have been made either to Los Angeles, Sacramento, San Francisco, or Portland."[241]

As the market shifted, so the lines of distinction between the Puritan companies began to blur. The local newspaper began referring to California Vegetable Growers for the first time in June 1943, stating that the firm was "affiliated with California Lettuce Growers."[242] In a matter of months, all mention of California Lettuce Growers was gone and the distinctions between California Produce and California Vegetable then began to haze over.

The papers continued to report the companies separately, but the companies' employees were both housed in the dorms and small homes built on the Blythe Ice lot. Both Fred Grande and Pete Compten stated in interviews that internally, people referred to the Puritan firms interchangeably, including California Produce, which when it arrived in Blythe was not a Puritan company. Reading between the lines, however, California Produce installed its own ice-making equipment in December 1943, creating an unwanted competitor to Puritan. By September of the next year, California Produce was suddenly "part of a cooperative" under California Vegetable. In the past, with firms such as Santa Barbara Ice and Ord Ice in Santa Barbara, this meant the competitor had been acquired by Puritan.

As the war wound down, Puritan had to be happy with the results. Every report on shipments started with "biggest," "largest" or "record." Annual proceeds for Blythe agricultural products topped $4.4 million, and more than half that volume was handled by Puritan's Blythe Ice.[243]

AIR LETTUCE

When the war ended, it was clear the training camp would be dismantled. Holding to the vision of ice transforming the ability to transport produce across long distances, Puritan created a publicity stunt at the end of the war, shipping produce to the East Coast by military aircraft.

On December 27, 1945, the *Palo Verde Times* reported:

> *A new era in out-of-season vegetable marketing from Palo Verde Valley is presaged by the airplane shipment of lettuce from Blythe today.*

> *Number 3 cargo plane of the Flying Tiger Line took off from an airport near the city shortly after noon with 8,000 pounds of fresh vegetables, including 4,000 pounds of winter lettuce, bound for the New York market. The entire shipment was made by the California Vegetable Growers. The lettuce heads were individually wrapped in cellophane, moisture-tight, and sealed with wing labels marked, "Airborne, Fresher, Better," and carrying the Bear Brand of California Vegetable Growers. There were four dozen heads to the crate, and 67 crates in the shipment. The other half of the cargo was loaded first, at Santa Maria. It consisted of about 12 creates each of pre-packaged cauliflower, broccoli, celery, artichokes, and strawberries.*
>
> *The schedule reads like something out of a dream. The field-ripened produce is cut and packed on a sunny December Wednesday in California. It is placed in an airplane Thursday, is unloaded in New York on Friday, is on the vegetable stands early Saturday morning, and is served by housewives and restaurants on Saturday evening and Sunday—where snow and ice lie on the streets. It is believed that buyers will gladly pay the 20 percent higher price allowed by the O.P.A.* [the United States Office of Price Administration] *for the difference in quality will make the produce cheaper at that price. If this is proved to be the case, today's experiment will become a regular part of the marketing program, not only of California Lettuce Growers, but also of other produce companies.*

The cargo plane was piloted by Joe Robert, one of Chenault's original Flying Tigers.[244]

Air-freight fresh produce, while enjoying a premium market to this day with firms like Harry and David, never took off as the significant means of transport Puritan had envisioned at the end of World War II.

The Reorg

As 1946 started, Puritan began a reorganization that would take over ten years to complete. Two factors seemed to drive the change. First, company co-founder T.P. Dalzell was not well. The company began to think about transitioning the firm into the hands of other officers. The second factor was the major shift in company proceeds from the Guadalupe–Santa Barbara axis to the fields and ice plant of Blythe.

T.P. Dalzell was divesting himself. In the spring of 1946, he sold the T.P. Ranch in the Santa Ynez Valley to General Jacob McGavock Dickinson. General Dickinson owned an Arabian horse breeding farm in Tennessee. In August of that year, Dickinson moved his family and sixty prized Arabians to his new ranch, which he renamed Traveler's Rest Ranch.

Then, starting a chapter of change for Puritan, founder T.P. Dalzell passed away on April 26, 1947, at his home in Palm Springs, California. He is interred at the Santa Barbara Cemetery.

At Puritan headquarters, Attorney Melvin "Mac" McCaughey (pronounced McCoy), with the firm since 1943 as a real estate specialist, was promoted to vice-president. Former Teamsters manager from Santa Maria, H. Don Underwood, was promoted to the general manager of Blythe Ice and California Lettuce/Vegetable/Produce and made a vice-president of the firm. This latter move sent Donald Dalzell back to the corporate office in Santa Barbara. "Mr. Underwood is now in Blythe acquainting himself with the produce organization's work. He has been with the association since its inception as assistant personnel and public relations manager, with headquarters at Guadalupe. He spent some time in Blythe during the melon harvests of 1944 and 1945. Mr. and Mrs. Underwood will move to Blythe early in March [1946] and make their home here."[245]

As soon as Underwood arrived, he launched an expansion plan for Blythe Ice, taking the plant to 335 tons per day. The year ended with local agricultural proceeds surpassing the $5 million mark and with Blythe Ice handling the bulk of the local ice business.

Underwood quickly made a home in the area, taking on roles as president of the Palo Verde Valley Vegetable Growers Association and eventually of the powerful Palo Verde Irrigation District. In 1962, a well-established community leader in Blythe by this point, Underwood became the president of the local Farmers & Merchants Bank.

In 1948, the paper would report that the Puritan dynasty in Blythe was still viable. Over sixteen million pounds of ice had been used in the month of June for the melon crop. "One of Palo Verde valley's biggest industries, and probably least advertised, is ice manufacturing...Blythe Ice Company is now operating full time manufacturing white ice for use by the Santa Fe in icing refrigerator cars at Winslow. The railway company's plant at Winslow cannot keep up with the midsummer demand."[246]

H. Don Underwood, holding shovel, and Richard Phillips at rear, at a Pepsi distributorship groundbreaking in Ventura, California, in 1965. *Bruce Phillips collection.*

But under Underwood's guidance, Blythe became something more than ice and produce. Underwood, working with his good friend Mac McCaughey, took Puritan in new directions in the valley. These directions proved to be the future of Puritan, but one thing needed to happen first.

Chapter 9

Meltwaters

Founder Leon Phillips passed away October 13, 1958, at his home on the Santa Barbara Riviera. His life had been full. He'd built a large, complex and successful corporate entity. He had served in World War I, and his company played a role in providing food and ice for both General Patton's Desert Training Center and for numerous military training camps, as well as for the cities around defense plants in Southern California.

Phillips knew how to enjoy himself. He owned a succession of motor yachts, and he and his wife, Blanche, traveled extensively in Europe and the United States. His two sons grew up to participate in Puritan and its subsidiaries, and son Donald became a concert clarinetist and launched his own music store and film company in Santa Barbara.

Both Phillips and Dalzell believed in ice. Puritan expanded into several new markets during the reign of the two founders. The company planted thousands of acres to lettuce, carrots, cauliflower, corn and cantaloupes. It built up the largest poultry farm on the planet. Through the acquisitions during World War II, the firm managed a chili dehydration plant and a large Chevrolet dealership and engine repair shop in Guadalupe. Then it built the vacuum pre-cooler there in 1952.

But all of these endeavors were founded on the fundamental requirement that the ice plants continue operating. While Dalzell and Phillips were alive, only the Atascadero ice plant closed. That plant, as its business dwindled, was geographically outside their area of influence and focus. The axis of power for Puritan was from Guadalupe through Lompoc and Santa Barbara

Leon Redner Phillips, 1958. *Bruce Phillips collection.*

to Blythe. In 1953, with the poultry farm long gone, the Atascadero plant was sold to Antone Ruso.

Then Leon Phillips died.

New lines of power were already in place. Leo McMahon, the attorney who brokered the purchase and leasing of Japanese companies in Guadalupe and who had been pivotal in the firm as it expanded into Blythe, had died in 1952 when his private plane flipped in an irrigation ditch during a landing in Sonora, Mexico. But two other men emerged as the clear leaders in the firm: Melvin "Mac" McCaughey and Don Underwood.

Mac McCaughey, a corporate vice-president, helped fuel the company's success in Blythe. According to John Rasmussen, who would become the final CEO of the firm in 1976, "Mac McCaughey acquired about 7,000 acres of farmland for Puritan [in the Blythe area], then sold off half of it for tax purposes. The land [in Blythe] was not owned by Puritan." It was owned by the families—the Phillipses, the Dalzells, the Marshalls and the McMahons. (Perry Marshall was Puritan's accountant.)

Rasmussen recalled, "Don Phillips used to ride down with me to Blythe, and one time he made a statement to me. He says, 'I don't know why my father gave half this land to these other two people.' I said, 'Don, he didn't give anything. He wouldn't have had anything. It took somebody else's imagination to even go down there.' Mac McCaughey purchased all this land down there."[247]

Though McCaughey was centered in Santa Barbara at this time, it was unanimous among the company officers that Don Underwood, still down in Blythe, would take the helm. This decision was supported by the Dalzell and Phillips heirs, both families with sons working as presidents and vice-presidents in the firm. Rasmussen would recall that "the younger generation never seemed to be much interested in the Puritan business operations." Though Don Phillips was perhaps the most involved, he would leave work during the day to practice with the symphony.

It was Don Underwood who had a vision for the future, and the future in his vision was an immediate one.

Within a matter of months, Puritan closed the Lompoc ice plant and sold the property it sat on and then spawned two new firms: Puritan Cattle, incorporated December 8, 1958, and Puritan Leasing, incorporated a year later. Between the two incorporations, the Underwoods moved back to Santa Barbara.

Puritan Cattle was an effort to capitalize on the upsurge in cattle ranching taking place in the Palo Verde Valley throughout the 1940s and '50s. Puritan owned a parcel of land on the inside of an elbow of the Colorado River where they grew vegetables. Land above and below its forty-acre parcel was a nearly unbroken string of cattle feedlots for a stretch of ten miles. Puritan threw up some fences, defined a niche by feeding alfalfa—a rotation crop from its fields—to four thousand calves it did not own and went into the feedlot business in a small way.

NEW LEASE ON LIFE

Puritan Leasing, on the other hand, was an outgrowth of Don Underwood's experience as a banker and of the rich experience within Puritan with the financing of agricultural start-ups.

Launched initially as a service corporation to help finance new agricultural ventures, the new firm quickly shifted focus. Headquartered in Santa Barbara, local companies that needed help financing equipment were the quickly expanding restaurant and hotel chains based in the area.

Puritan Leasing leased a wide array of vehicles, equipment and even buildings to a variety of firms. Early lessees included Motel 6 and Sambo's Restaurants, and piggybacking on the success of these two businesses, Puritan Leasing expanded across the country. The firm leased to farming operations, restaurants, grocery stores and other businesses. "We leased a tuna trawler," Rasmussen recalled. The trawler kept going astray, however, and would end up picking up drugs and bullet holes in Panama rather than tuna off the coast of Monterey.[248]

Puritan Leasing quickly grew to an interstate business as it followed its clients into Oregon, Nevada and Arizona, eventually ending up in eighteen states. In California, offices opened in Anaheim, Fresno, Los Angeles, Sacramento, San Diego, San Francisco and San Jose.

But Underwood continued to cast about aggressively for new opportunities. On March 26, 1962, in a simple transaction that would alter the fate of the company, Underwood acquired the Pepsi-Cola bottling plants and distribution rights for Ventura and southern Santa Barbara Counties. With ice seeming less and less relevant, Puritan leased out a portion of the Santa Barbara ice plant to C.T. Johnson of Artesia Water a few months later.

With these transitions from utilitarian ice and produce company to something grander and based more on making good impressions, another transition was in order. Puritan bought land at the corner of Anacapa and Arrellaga Streets in Santa Barbara and built a respectable, two-story, Spanish-style headquarters.

John Rasmussen started with Puritan Leasing in 1965, just as the company was moving into its new offices. Ice manufacturing was still underway in Santa Barbara but would cease for good a year later. The Rasmussens had owned a chick hatchery, a poultry farm, a feed business, a prefab building business and a portable mill in Iowa. But their customers were leaving the farms and taking forty-hour-a-week jobs. Pulling up their stakes in Iowa and coming west without work, the Rasmussens drove through Blythe. "It was

Palo Verde Equipment, 1984. *Bruce Phillips collection.*

120 degrees. I told my wife, 'I never want to see this place again.'" In Santa Barbara, he applied for an open position as field representative for Puritan Leasing, a new role for the company. "First thing they did was send me to Blythe. I couldn't understand why people were there. I think some of them must have run out of gas and run out of money at the same time and they just ended up staying there."[249]

In 1970, Puritan added San Luis Obispo and northern Santa Barbara Counties to its Pepsi distribution company. Then, in 1971, it bought out Broadway Farm Equipment in Blythe and renamed it Palo Verde Equipment, selling and leasing International Harvester trucks, tractors and other farm equipment.

While activity continued in Blythe (and less so in Guadalupe), the focal point of the Puritan Companies shifted once again to Santa Barbara. Blythe sales with Blythe Ice and Palo Verde Equipment companies reached $2 million in 1973. Santa Barbara–based businesses, in particular Puritan Leasing and the Pepsi-Cola distributorship, brought in $11 million.

CLOSING CHAPTERS

Both Mac McCaughey and Don Underwood retired in 1976, and John Rasmussen, by then residing in Santa Barbara and the clear leader in the firm, took the helm. The firm was running smoothly at this point with proceeds topping $15 million annually.

The integration of the companies was key throughout the firm's existence. Early synergies had existed between California Lettuce and Puritan Ice and then Puritan Poultry and Puritan Ice. Now, Palo Verde Equipment stood at the center of a complex web of relationships. It provided equipment when Puritan Leasing leased farm equipment. It supplied Pepsi with semis, delivery trucks, pickups and other equipment. "We had forty-eight [Pepsi] routes, plus the big semis," Rasmussen recalled. Then, when leased vehicles returned to Puritan after tours of duty with their customers, Puritan put them on the Palo Verde Equipment lot and sold them.

In addition, the companies all operated against different accounting year ends so that Pepsi might expense a dozen new trucks as their year began, while infusing Palo Verde Equipment with a large sale at year end, giving the various companies tax advantages.

There were problems collecting from leasing customers, issues with land titles in Blythe and labor troubles at the vacuum pre-cooling plant, but for the most part, when John Scully, CEO of Pepsi-Co in 1983, asked Rasmussen at a Pepsi distributors meeting in Palm Springs, "Are you interested in selling?' Rasmussen could answer honestly, "I really didn't think so. Everything is going fine."

But Don Phillips, standing with them, asked, "What's it worth?"

At the time, Pepsi was consolidating its distributorships, a profit-laden end of the business that it wanted to bring in-house. As Pepsi-Co's interest in consolidating distributors became known, other buyers emerged. Rasmussen recalled, "We had inquiries from London, New York, Florida and Minnesota which were [firms] all involved with multiple [Pepsi] franchises. Minnesota had thirty-three franchises. Within, it must have been no more than a week or so, we had inquiries from every one of them."

Back at the home office, the writing was on the wall. "It was, 'You buy us or we buy you.'" Puritan began the process of merging some of its companies.

Palo Verde Equipment was leased to another International Harvester dealer in 1975. Blythe Ice was sold to a cooperative of the ice company's customers calling themselves Hi-Value Processors. Hi-Value ran the firm,

John Rasmussen, former and final CEO of the Puritan companies, 2010. *Photo by David Petry.*

making three-hundred-pound blocks of ice and loading rail cars, but increasingly trucks, until it in turn sold out to Fisher Ranch of the Palo Verde Valley. Fisher purchased the site after its packing sheds and offices nearby burned to the ground in a 2003 fire. Fisher continued making ice until 2008, when a new, more efficient chipped ice machine was installed. The company still operates the site, running melons, lettuce and other produce through a fully modern packing and pre-cooling plant.

In 1976, Puritan closed the vacuum pre-cooling plant in Guadalupe after labor troubles became too much of a drain on the firm's energies. California Vegetable had been absorbed by California Lettuce by the end of the 1950s, and Puritan dropped leases as they expired in the Santa Maria and Blythe Valleys. The cattle feed lot property, an environmental liability because of its proximity to the Colorado River, was donated to the County of Riverside in the early 1980s and converted a year later by the county into a public park: McIntyre Park.

In 1984, James Lindsey, a Pepsi distributor based in Bakersfield, made an offer for the entire company, and pushed by the heirs of the founding families, Puritan's board accepted the offer.

Almost.

"The sale was put together the first time in '84," Rasmussen said. "Negotiations had been put together. Everything had been agreed upon. The papers were at the law office. Everyone was there to sign. Attorneys from the buyers, the sellers. Everybody's sitting around in an office. And nothing was done.

"Ted Dalzell, Jr. [grandson of T.P.] was there, and he finally said, 'If you guys haven't got any more important things to do, I've got something I want to do.' So he left."

And so the deal fell apart.

Almost.

Employees at the firm suspected something was in the wind. The board and company officers started to hold meetings in secret at various locations, including the San Ysidro Ranch. They kept the ongoing discussions around the sale quiet, though there were inklings among the staff.

"Two years later, we sold it to the same people," Rasmussen said. "For a lot more money."

When they sat down again in 1986, they put ink on the papers and Puritan Ice, Puritan Leasing, the Pepsi distributorships and some land in Blythe—all that was left of the Puritan quiver of firms—were sold for "a substantial sum." No one was willing to say, even twenty-five years later, how much.[250]

Postscript

Telling the Puritan Story

The telling of this story has had a life of its own. It began in January 2010 when model train enthusiast and builder Ken Kelley of Santa Ynez contacted John Fritsche in Santa Barbara. Having built a beautiful one-eighth-scale replica of the Santa Barbara train station and the old Railway Express building (most recently Open Air Bicycles), he wanted pictures of the old Southern Pacific roundhouse. John got those for him.

Then Ken wanted pictures of the old ice plant, Puritan Ice.

John had not been aware of the plant, though it stood on Cabrillo Boulevard for many years after his arrival in town. Attracted to anything mechanical and technical and always there to help with old pictures of Santa Barbara, John started to dig around. On the web, squirreled away in a personal account in the photo-sharing site Flickr, he found a pair of images. One, of a building exterior, was labeled "Puritan Ice, original ice plant, SB, 1920s." The second, an interior shot, was labeled "Puritan Ice, making ice—SB ice plant, 1930s."

Intrigued, John began tracking down Puritan. Over the coming months, John would involve me in the project, his curiosity driving mine. We would find out that Bruce Phillips, grandson of Leon Phillips, had posted those two images and that the interior shot could have been either Santa Barbara or Guadalupe, so nearly identical were the interiors, and the exterior was of Puritan Ice in Atascadero.

Atascadero plant as it looked in 2010. *Photo by Connie Pillsbury.*

In Atascadero, the old ice plant still stands but is now an auto shop. The rail spur beside it is no more than an empty right of way. We found this out by dropping ourselves in front of the current building via Google Street View, a project that has photographed millions of miles of roadways across the planet. As we dug into the story in Atascadero, we contacted Connie Pillsbury, a local writer and historian. She sounded interested but then went quiet. Worried, we poked at her by e-mail, and she responded, saying she had more things to look into. About the time we were ready to give up on getting details on Atascadero, we received a fifty-odd-page notebook from Connie in the mail with copies of articles of incorporation, *Atascadero News* articles, photographs, maps and more.

The notebook was a treasure-trove for Puritan's chapter in Atascadero.

Lompoc was also thorny. Sitting on the outskirts of town and fairly small, people didn't remember the plant. Then we found Karen Paaske at the Lompoc Historical Society who sent us to Don and Minnie Stalker—Minnie is the daughter of Puritan Lompoc's second and final manager, Sam Hoover—and to Bill Rule, whose father owned and operated Lompoc Ice Company. Then Karen unearthed articles about Puritan from the local newspaper, the *Lompoc Record*, and in a matter of two or three days transcribed the many articles straight to e-mail for us. As this book came together, Karen helped gather images. Violet McNett, former owner of the property, was also extremely helpful.

Another amazing trove.

In April 2010, John Fritsche and I visited the Guadalupe plant with Rennie Pili, the current owner of the property. Behind locked gates and a fading façade, the ice-making machinery was still in the plant and the tanks were still full of brine. Redwood planking, a full twelve inches in width, lined the inner walls of the storage buildings with a thick layer of dark Portuguese cork behind it. A barn owl lived in the tallest of the buildings. The old icing platform, 458 feet long, had been razed.

Apio now runs the main vegetable packing facility in Guadalupe. Its products are fresh, mixed vegetable trays with a sealed container of ranch dressing dip in the center. It sells to Costco, Ralph's and Vons, and the company pre-cools and ships in refrigerated trucks.

"They're planning to build a housing tract across the road to the south here," Pili, former mayor of Guadalupe explained. "When they do, we'll see what we want to do with the Puritan site."

When I returned to Guadalupe in September 2010, I met John Perry, owner of Guadalupe Napa Auto Parts and a collector of Guadalupe memorabilia. He generously shared his time and memories, and his collection of local produce labels.

Then, in October 2011, the old Guadalupe plant was demolished. Owner Rennie Pili felt it was the right thing to do. The old plant was a hazard and was becoming an eyesore. There were no immediate plans for the property, though there were several unsolicited proposals for it. The property is zoned for industrial use with a commercial overlay, so there are many options.

In Blythe, where I visited in July 2010, the ice plant still stands. Old rail spurs slip under tumbleweed and sand, unused. Kathy Cusick, of Fisher Ranch, gave me a tour of the place. Her grandmother, Jeanette Hyduke, a local history expert and writer for the *Palo Verde Times*, hooked us up. In the

Interior, Puritan Ice, Guadalupe plant #2, 2010. *Photo by David Petry.*

Exterior, Puritan Ice, Guadalupe plant #2 during demolition, October 2011. *Photo by Rennie Pili.*

Artist's rendering of Puritan Ice, Santa Barbara plant #1, circa 1950. *Patrick Berg, artist.*

old buildings, mostly disused, are the old compressors. The only indication that the plant was not of the standard Puritan provenance was the sign high on a column stating that the plant was built by Associated Refrigeration Engineers of Los Angeles. Puritan, when it built new, used Gay Engineering from 1922 through to the 1952 vacuum pre-cooling plant. Associated Refrigeration Engineers was an offshoot of Gay Engineering opened by ex-employees. This small piece of evidence indicates that the plant was, in fact, purchased, dismantled and shipped to Blythe from elsewhere.

During my visit, a small crew was sitting at the Fisher Ranch intake door where the last of the season's cantaloupes would appear at any minute, a snaking conveyor system spreading out behind them that would grade and label and pack the cantaloupes. The conveyors filled the vast space with complex order. "This is all going away," Kathy Cusick explained. "They're putting in a whole new system starting tomorrow."

Before I left Blythe, I spent two long afternoons at the Palo Verde Historical Museum with Sylvia Summers going through their bound issues of the *Palo Verde Times*. In the *Times* we found another excellent trove of information on Puritan's stay in town.

The missing piece in our research was still Santa Barbara. Ken Kelley still needed a picture of the plant, and we still had not found one. The plant was razed in 1991 as part of the Fess Parker Plaza Hotel projects. In the name of preservation, as-built blueprints were made and photographs taken. The place had most recently been used as a plywood warehouse. The photos were of a ruined shell. Former city historian Jake Jacobus helped us get access to the photos and plans.

At least we knew dimensions. But we still wanted to "see" it.

We finally contacted architect and artist Patrick Berg and asked him to draw us a representation of the plant based on what we knew. Patrick created the Santa Barbara Puritan Ice plant for us for the first time.

Only later did I think to knock on the door of the old Phillips' homestead on the Riviera in Santa Barbara. Connie Phillips, widow of Donald Phillips, answered the door and welcomed me in. In her photo albums, we found three images of Puritan in Santa Barbara, two very early, of the plant before rail icing platforms were built, when the company was marketing Hughes Ice Cream. The third was later, taken from Cabrillo Boulevard, with the icing platform barely discernable through the trees.

She gave me her nephew Bruce Phillips's phone number—son of Richard Phillips and grandson of L.R.—and a circle closed. Bruce had posted the images on Flickr and had been unsure about what they depicted. He thought they were of Santa Barbara since this had been the firm's first and most central plant. Bruce was extremely helpful and provided numerous other images and many recollections about the company.

The most enjoyable aspect of the project was my association with John Fritsche. John's specialty is the history of technology and the institutions that develop it. A recent project had been researching the founding years of the Loughead Aircraft Company (now named Lockheed) in Santa Barbara. John is patient, persistent and always curious. John and I pursued our own paths through this story, each sometimes thinking the other was following an empty or at least peripheral trail through the past. Invariably, we would find ourselves crossing each other's paths and asking each other for briefings and copies and updates. We both ended up in places we would never have found alone.

Throughout, we shared a timeline in the form of a spreadsheet. It contained dates and descriptions and sources for everything we touched. We would make our entries in different colors so we could identify the changes at the weekly or monthly moments when the timelines merged. By the end, the timeline contained over one thousand entries.

Puritan Ice, Santa Barbara, as it appeared before demolition in 1991. *City of Santa Barbara.*

John Fritsche (left) and Bruce Phillips review collected historical materials in 2010. *Photo by David Petry.*

PUBLICATION NOTES

It is also important to point out that this work was driven purely by curiosity. Neither John nor I were funded in any way, nor were the researchers who helped us. Thus, this history is unauthorized. No one from Puritan or the families of the heirs has in any way approved this book (though Bruce Phillips' and Rennie Pili's help and encouragement were invaluable). The words are my own, as are the conclusions that are not contained in quotation marks. John Fritsche certainly helped me reach many of them, but as written, I take full responsibility.

HOLES IN THE ICE

Traveling through the years as a historian with any firm is likely to be frustrating. If you have full access to the company papers, you see into the depths of the firm. But the past has a way of covering its tracks.

Puritan's papers reside with its law firm, a firm whose first customer was Puritan. We were refused access to any and all files at the firm through the intervention of the Dalzell heirs.

We could cast a pall over Puritan by assuming this blocking of access had a reason, that perhaps Puritan's treatment of the Japanese in the Santa Maria Valley was not its darkest hour. Puritan was embroiled in labor issues, contract disputes and tax cases. Many cases ended up in court and therefore the public record. But companies hire lawyers, and lawyers need to keep busy like the rest of us, and it seems likely that Puritan was no more or less legally contentious or morally disingenuous than other firms of the day.

But as a result, a complete timeline of the firm and its companies, its legal proceedings and its critical decisions is therefore impossible.

There were other resources that did not turn up in our searches. Very little memorabilia of the Puritan companies surfaced. We found a handful of images and some egg carton and produce labels. We found an ice pick. There were the three standing plants. But for the most part, photographs and physical objects relating to the firm were rare or nonexistent.

We also hoped to find in some form the words of the founders. The two men remain elusive. Their business or personal correspondence would have

Exterior door, Puritan Ice, Guadalupe plant #2, 2010. *Photo by David Petry.*

Exterior, Blythe Ice, Blythe, 2010. *Photo by David Petry.*

been an invaluable insight into their lives. They spent decades together in a set of small, utilitarian offices upstairs above their original ice plant. They achieved a surprising reach of business with surprising success, with surprising leaps of faith and insight.

Yet they remain aloof.

What we are left with remains a surprisingly clear picture of a company that created a lifeline of ice in Santa Barbara and San Luis Obispo Counties and, later, in Riverside County and then fed that lifeline with fresh produce and eggs from farms that did not exist when the ice plants first arrived. Their plans took advantage of wide-open windows of opportunity, but wide open or not, they acted boldly in an arena where the odds were always stacked against them.

Their impact on the places where they did business was immense. The people who fed their ice plants with products became millionaires in a time when that was rare. Even the Japanese who supplied Puritan and were excluded from direct ownership of land and other assets became wealthy.

The biggest transformation, though, was to create a demand and a market for fresh produce from these areas. The farms in those valleys today are reliant on a structure and relationships that Puritan put into place nearly ninety years ago, even if the need for fresh ice has long since melted away.

Notes

Chapter 1

1. Interview with Melvin Hammel, February 27, 2010, former employee of Carol Johnson, last contract delivery service with Puritan Ice in Santa Barbara.
2. Clyde Hendricks, *Puritan Companies Celebrate Fifty Years in Business*, December 1972. Puritan Companies Press Release.
3. *Santa Barbara News-Press*, "Puritan Ice Co.—Complex Operation," July 21, 1962.
4. *ICC Docket 2613*, SP control of CP, approved February 6, 1923 (76 ICC 508), http://utahrails.net/ogden/ogden-sp.php.
5. Don Strack, "Ogden Rails," 2005, Union Pacific Historical Society, http://utahrails.net/ogden/ogden-sp.php.
6. *The Union Pacific Railroad, 1900*, http://www.history-map.com/picture/004/Railroad-Pacific-Union-The.htm.
7. Don L. Hofsommer, *The Southern Pacific, 1901–1985* (College Station, Texas: Texas A&M University Press, 1986), 13. (http://utahrails.net/ogden/ogden-sp.php.)
8. Population History of Los Angeles from 1890–1990, http://physics.bu.edu/~redner/projects/population/cities/la.html.; Richard L. Forstall, ed., *California: Population of Counties by Decennial Census: 1900 to 1990*, Population Division, U.S. Bureau of the Census. (20233http://www.census.gov/population/cencounts/ca190090.txt.).

9. "Timeline of San Diego History," https://www.sandiegohistory.org/timeline/timeline2.htm.
10. "Gustavus Franklin Swift," http://en.wikipedia.org/wiki/Gustavus_Franklin_Swift.
11. Anthony W. Thompson, Robert J. Church and Bruce H. Jones, *Pacific Fruit Express*, Second Edition, (Wilton, CA: Signature Press, 1992).
12. Phone conversation, Ted Dalzell with author, May 25, 2010.
13. Michael James Phillips, *The History of Santa Barbara County*, Vol. II (Chicago: S.J. Clarke, 1927), 100.
14. *Santa Barbara News-Press*, "Puritan Ice Co."
15. *Charleston Daily Mail*, "Mr. Mars Has a Date with Old Mother Earth This Evening," June 18, 1922.
16. "Constance Savage Keith Lowell," Lowell Observatory Research, http://www.lowell.edu/Research/library/paper/c_lowell.html.
17. William Lowell Putnam, *Percival Lowell's Big Red Car* (Jefferson, NC: Mcfarland & Co. Inc. Publishing, 2002), 159.
18. *Ice and Refrigeration Annual*, Vol. 63 (Chicago: Nickerson and Collins Co., 1922), 37.
19. *Morning Press*, December 28, 1922.

Chapter 2

20. John Steinbeck, *East of Eden* (New York: Penguin Group, 1952), 435.
21. Richard J. Orsi, *Sunset Limited* (Berkeley: University of California Press, 2005), 317–38.
22. Thompson, Church and Jones, *Pacific Fruit Express*.
23. Kent Edward Haldan, "Our Japanese Citizens: A Study of Race, Class, and Ethnicity in Three Japanese American Communities in Santa Barbara County, 1900–1960" (PhD diss., UC Berkeley, spring 2000), 131.
24. "California Lettuce Growers, Incorporated, Articles of Incorporation," State of California, July 25, 1923.
25. Vada F. Carlson, *This Is Our Valley (Santa Maria)* (Santa Maria: Santa Maria Valley Historical Society, 1959), 236.
26. Walter Docker interview, January 7, 2010; Rennie Pili interview, March 26, 2010.
27. Alexander James Wallis-Tayler, *The Pocket Book of Refrigeration and Ice Making* (London: Norman W. Henley Publishing Co., 1905), 100–14; A.E.

Beales, Process of Making Ice, United States Patent 959697, May 31, 1910; G.T. Vorhees, Ice Making Process, United States Patent 1322660, November 25, 1919.

28. Details of operations derived from: Interview, Walter Docker, January 7, 2010, former employee, Puritan Ice Company, Santa Barbara plant, mid-1930s, by John Fritsche; Interview, Pete Compten, February 25, 2010, former employee, Blythe Ice Company, late 1940s with author; Interview, Rennie Pili, March 26, 2010, former employee and current co-owner of Puritan Ice Company of Guadalupe, over thirty years association with the Guadalupe plant.
29. R.D. Van Valkenbrgh, Ice Conveyor and Elevator, United States Patent 1049623, January 7, 1913.
30. Carlson, *This Is Our Valley*, 236.
31. *Los Angeles Times*, "Farm News of the Great Southwest," April 26, 1925.
32. "Guadalupe," California Japantowns, http://www.californiajapantowns.org/guadalupe.html.
33. Naomi Hirahara, *An American Son: The Story of George Aratani* (Los Angeles: Japanese American National Museum, 2001), 1–23.
34. Ibid.
35. *Santa Barbara Morning Press*, "Puritan Ice Company and Allied Industries," August 8, 1927.
36. Ibid.

CHAPTER 3

37. Stella Haverland Rouse, "A Lack of Ice," *Santa Barbara News-Press*, November 14, 1965.
38. Ibid.
39. Stella Haverland Rouse, "Santa Barbara Ice Companies," *Santa Barbara News-Press*, July 21, 1968.
40. *Los Angeles Times*, "Santa Ana Moving to Secure an Ice Plant," May 5, 1894.
41. First Presbyterian Church, *History of the First Presbyterian Church* (Morristown, NJ: Banner Steam Print, 1880), 164.
42. Joan M. Williams, *Morristown* (Charleston, SC: Arcadia Publishing, 1996), 116.
43. *Los Angeles Times*, "Santa Barbara County," February 6, 1895.
44. *Los Angeles Times*, "Ice in San Bernardino," February 2, 1899.

45. *Los Angeles Times*, "The Development of the Southwest," March 5, 1899.
46. *Los Angeles Times*, "Ice Companies in Court War in Santa Barbara," December 18, 1924.
47. *Los Angeles Times*, "Condensed Coldness, What the Union Ice Company Is Doing in Los Angeles," February 28, 1886.
48. Rouse, "A Lack of Ice."
49. Cassius M. Gay, Ice Making Apparatus, Patent 1273055, United States Patent Office, July 16, 1918.
50. *Oxnard Daily Courier*, "Oxnard and Vicinity," June 27, 1922.
51. For this and many other events where Puritan's fate and future was defined in legal terms, information was not available. The law firm of Mullins and Henzel, the continuation of the law firm that Phillips and Dalzell used throughout the development of Puritan Ice, refused access to company records even though Puritan has been defunct for over twenty years. Refusal on the instructions of Ted Dalzell, grandson of founder T.P. Dalzell.
52. *Santa Barbara News-Press*, June 11, 1925.

CHAPTER 4

53. Charles Montville Gidney, Benjamin Brooks and Edwin M. Sheridan, "Emmett G. Ord," *History of Santa Barbara, San Luis Obispo and Ventura Counties*, Vol. 2 (Chicago: Lewis Publishing Co., 1917), 661–63.
54. Ibid.
55. *Los Angeles Times*, "Farm News of the Southwest, May Plant Lettuce," November 18, 1923.
56. *Los Angeles Times*, "Ventura Vegetable Growers Hold Tour," December 23, 1923.
57. *Los Angeles Times*, "Most Prosperous Year in Ventura County's History."
58. *Oxnard Daily Courier*, "Ord Ice Company advertisement for Ice Delivery," July 14, 1923.
59. *Oxnard Daily Courier*, "News Notes of People in Camarillo District," July 21, 1923.
60. *Oxnard Daily Courier*, "Ord Ice Co. to Build Big Ice Plant and Vegetable Packing Houses Here, on Enterprise Street," September 25, 1923.
61. *Oxnard Daily Courier*, "Roy Guyer Awarded Contract to Build Ord Ice Co. Plant," October 2, 1923.
62. *Oxnard Daily Courier*, "Machinery Soon to Be Installed in Plant of Ord Ice Co. Here," October 5, 1923.

63. *Oxnard Daily Courier*, "Ord Ice Co. Operating; to Have Ice Wednesday," January 5, 1924.
64. *Oxnard Daily Courier*, "Employee of Ice Co. Drops Dead at Work," May 3, 1924.
65. *Oxnard Daily Courier*, "Union Ice Buys Site for Ice Plant Near Railroad," May 9, 1924.
66. *San Francisco Chronicle*, "The Ice Monopoly," June 11, 1885.
67. *San Francisco Chronicle*, "Incorporations," December 31, 1882.
68. *San Francisco Chronicle*, "A Freeze-Out Suit, Operations of the Local Ice Monopoly," May 13, 1885, pg 1.
69. *Los Angeles Times*, "The Union Ice Company," January 15, 1886.
70. *Los Angeles Times*, "Ice Picks and Guns Used in Savage Ice War," July 6, 1936.
71. *Los Angeles Times*, "The Ice Trust, Letters to the Times," June 8, 1890.
72. *Oxnard Daily Courier*, "Union Ice Buys Site for Ice Plant Near Railroad," May 9, 1924.
73. *Los Angeles Times*, "Oxnard Going in Heavily for Vegetable Production," June 29, 1924.
74. *Los Angeles Times*, "Irrigation Brings Change of Crops," June 8, 1924.
75. *Woodland Democrat*, "Dixon Ice Plant With Agency Here Sells to Union Ice; New Prices," August 21, 1924, Evening Edition.
76. *Oakland Tribune*, "Ice Factory to Be Constructed at Watsonville," August 10, 1924.
77. *Los Angeles Times*, "Ice Firm to Build Two New Plants," October 19, 1924.
78. *Oxnard Daily Courier*, "Puritan Ice Co. to Buy Out Ord Ice, Deal Now Under Way," October 21, 1924.
79. *Oxnard Daily Courier*, "New Deal Between Ice Companies Under Way by Mission Ice Co.," October 29, 1924.
80. *Oxnard Daily Courier*, "Ord and Puritan Ice Companies Combined," October 1, 1925.
81. *Oxnard Daily Courier*, Ord Ice advertisement, June 11, 1926.
82. Ibid., June 29, 1926.
83. *Oxnard Daily Courier*, "Ord Ice Enjoys Good Business Year; Big Increase Noted," June 28, 1926.
84. *Los Angeles Times*, "Company Merger: Ice Concerns in Ventura County to Be Under One Head," November 7, 1926.
85. *Oxnard Daily Courier*, "Improvements to Ice Plant Completed Soon," January 10, 1928.

86 *Oxnard Daily Courier*, "Ords Will Erect a Plant in South," January 14, 1927.

CHAPTER 5

87. L.W. Allan, *Atascadero: The Vision of One—The Work of Many* (Tempe, AZ: Miracle Book Company, 2008), 13.
88. Ibid., 15–18.
89. Ibid., 18.
90. Ibid., 46–49.
91. Marguerite A. Travis, *The Birth of Atascadero* (Atascadero, CA: Travis, 2005), 70.
92. *Atascadero News*, "Packing House in Atascadero for Producers," January 6, 1922.
93. *Atascadero News*, "Cold Storage Plant Assured," April 14, 1922.
94. Ibid.
95. *Atascadero News*, "Cold Storage Plant Springs Up Like Magic," May 5, 1922; *Atascadero News*, "Cold Storage Plant Is Near Completion," June 2, 1922.
96. *Atascadero News*, "Storage Plant Has Begun Its Ice Delivery," July 28, 1922.
97. *Atascadero News*, "Atascadero Is Safe from the Fruit Tie-Up," August 18, 1922.
98. *Atascadero News*, "Cold Storage Saved Atascadero Fruit," November 10, 1922.
99. *Atascadero News*, "Storage Plant Now Operating at Full Capacity," September 21, 1923.
100. *Atascadero News*, "Cold Storage Plant Has Large Shipments," November 2, 1923.
101. Allan, *Atascadero*, 75.
102. Ibid.
103. *Los Angeles Times*, "Bankrupt Plea Filed by Lewis," December 31, 1924.
104. Allan, *Atascadero*, 75.
105. *Los Angeles Times*, "Will Appraise Lewis Assets," May 6, 1925; *Los Angeles Times*, "Lewis Case Creditors Vote Sale," December 15, 1925.
106. *Atascadero News*, "He Does Things!," September 18, 1925.
107. *Atascadero News*, "New Group to Buy Ice Plant at Atascadero," May 7, 1926.

108. *Atascadero News*, "Fruit Shipping Breaks Record in Atascadero," July 30, 1926.
109. *Atascadero News*, "Puritan Plant Storage Pears Give Surprise," December 26, 1926.
110. *Atascadero News*, "New Group to Buy Ice Plant at Atascadero," May 7, 1926.
111. *Woodland Democrat*, "Many Changes Made in Davis Farm Faculty," November 13, 1919.
112. Ralph Barrows Easson, *California Poultry Production* (San Francisco: Pacific Rural Press, 1923), 48.
113. *Van Nuys News*, "Culling Sessions with Easson," August 20, 1920.
114. *Los Angeles Times*, "Farm News," August 13, 1921.
115. *Woodland Democrat*, "Poultry Farmers Get a Lesson," August 24, 1921.
116. Easson, *California Poultry Production*, 42.
117. *Los Angeles Times*, "Ice Company Goes into Poultry Business," January 2, 1927.
118. *Atascadero News*, "Puritan Group Will Increase Plant in 1927," January 7, 1927.
119. *Atascadero News*, "Witmer-Puritan to Build Units to 90,000 Hens," February 4, 1927.
120. *Atascadero News*, "Puritan Plant Sets New Goal of 100,000 Hens," February 25, 1927.
121. *Atascadero News*, "5,000 Roosters to Be Brooded at Atascadero," March 18, 1927.
122. *Atascadero News*, "San Luis Men Inspect Plants in Atascadero," June 17, 1927.
123. *Atascadero News*, "Experts Praise Poultry Plants at Atascadero," July 15, 1927.
124. *Atascadero News*, "Puritan Plant Holds Schedule in Construction," August 5, 1927.
125. *Atascadero News*, "Puritan Plant Hatching Plans to Start Soon," September 9, 1927.
126. *Atascadero News*, "Eggs in Storage in Puritan Plant Number 15 Cars," June 1, 1928.
127. Puritan Ice Company brochure, circa 1929, John Rasmussen collection.
128. *Atascadero News*, "Dalzell Sees Bright Future at Atascadero," June 8, 1928.
129. *Atascadero News*, "Pacific Produce Begins Business at Atascadero," March 18, 1927.
130. Allan, *Atascadero*, 79.

131. *Los Angeles Times*, "They're Coming Back: That Livid 'Black Eye' That Atascadero Wore Is Fading Under an Egg and Fruit Treatment, October 27, 1929.
132. Ibid.
133. *Los Angeles Times*, "Easson Sees Good Future for Poultry," October 24, 1930.
134. *Woodland Democrat*, "Time Limit Nears for Signup in Rice Plan," June 19, 1936.
135. *Journal of the Senate*, Legislature of the State of California, Vol 1, June 30, 1946, 1.
136. Kingsley Smith, *History of Kimber Farms Inc.*, 2007, 11. http://www.hendrix-genetics.com/en/About-Us/History/Institut%20Selection%20Animal%20BV%20ISA/~/media/Files/ISA/History/History%20of%20Kimber%20Farms%20Inc%20USA.ashx

CHAPTER 6

137. Santa Barbara County deeds.
138. *Lompoc Record*, "PURITAN ICE COMPANY $85,000 Program Here," December 20, 1929.
139. *Lompoc Record*, "W.W. Broughton's Grandson Visits Lompoc, Bo Poertner," October 30, 2003.
140. Wikipedia, "John Bartholomew Gough," http://en.wikipedia.org/wiki/John_Bartholomew_Gough
141. E. Tucker, *History of Randolph County, Indiana* (Chicago: A.L. Kingman, 1882), 166.
142. Massachusetts Temperance Alliance, *Twenty-Third Annual Report*, September 30, 1874, 26–28.
143. Ibid.
144. Laurence W. Spanne, Cultural Resources Study, City of Lompoc General Plan Update Program, October 1988, 8.
145. Lompoc Historical Society, *Historical Ramblings*, http://www.lompochistory.org/user/temperance.pdf.
146. City of Lompoc Hanbook for Commission, Committee and Board Members, March 2008, 4.
147. Spanne, Cultural Resources Study, 6–9.
148. Lompoc Historical Society, *Historical Ramblings*: *Lompoc's Agricultural Legacy*. http://www.lompochistory.org/user/agricultural%20legacy.pdf.

149. City of Lompoc Handbook for Commission, Committee and Board Members, March 2008, 4.
150. Lompoc Historical Society, *Historical Ramblings: Lompoc's Agricultural Legacy*. http://www.lompochistory.org/user/agricultural%20legacy.pdf.
151. City of Lompoc Handbook for Commission, Committee and Board Members, March 2008, 4.
152. Statistical Report, California State Board of Agriculture, 1903, 386.
153. Lompoc Historical Society, *Historical Ramblings: Lompoc's Agricultural Legacy*. http://www.lompochistory.org/user/agricultural%20legacy.pdf.
154. *Los Angeles Times*, "State Leads in Flower Seed Production," March 21, 1926.
155. Lompoc Historical Society, *Historical Ramblings: Lompoc's Agricultural Legacy*. http://www.lompochistory.org/user/agricultural%20legacy.pdf.
156. *Lompoc Record*, "PURITAN ICE COMPANY."
157. *Lompoc Record*, "Vegetable Packing Sheds Are Center of Much Activity," August 26, 1937.
158. *Lompoc Record*, "PURITAN ICE COMPANY."
159. *Lompoc Record*, "Construction Steel for Ice Plant Is Here," January 3, 1930.
160. *Lompoc Record*, "Motive Power for Ice Plant Arrives and Is Installed," February 7, 1930.
161. *Lompoc Record*, "Puritan Ice Company 50 Ton Plant in Production," March 7, 1930.
162. *Lompoc Record*, "Valley Vegetables Being Shipped in Large Quantities," March 21, 1930.
163. *Lompoc Record*, "Puritan Ice Plant Now Shipping Two Car Loads of Ice Per Day to Guadalupe for Vegetable Packing," April 4, 1930.
164. *Lompoc Record*, "Installation of More Equipment Is Ice Co. Project," May 16, 1930.
165. *Lompoc Record*, "Locally-Made Ice Now Being Used Throughout City," July 11, 1930.
166. *Lompoc Record*, "Below Zero Weather Registered at Local Ice Concern's Plant," August 27, 1937.
167. *Lompoc Record*, "Ice Company to Build Large Storage Shed," November 5, 1937.
168. Raymond Ellis, "Farm News of the Great Southwest," *Los Angeles Times*, October 14, 1928.
169. Raymond Ellis, "Lompoc Valley Provides Real 'Wallop' to the Jaded Palate," *Los Angeles Times*, October 14, 1928.

170. Raymond Ellis, "Truck Crops Pay," *Los Angeles Times*, June 8, 1930.
171. "Rancho Oso History," http://www.ranchooso.net/rohistory.html.
172. *Coconino Sun*, September 16, 1938.
173. Putnam, *Big Red Car*, 161.
174. Ibid., 162–64.
175. Wisconsin Historical Society, "Federal Highway Act," http://www.wisconsinhistory.org/archstories/late_roads/fed_hwy_act.asp.
176. Wessel's Living History Farm, "Revolution in Transportation," http://www.livinghistoryfarm.org/farminginthe40s/money_14.html.
177. "Clarence Birdseye: Father of Frozen Food," History of Birds Eye, http://www.birdseyefoods.com/inspiration/pages/history.aspx.
178. Ibid.
179. Ibid.
180. Interview with Bill Rule, April 24, 2010.
181. Ibid.
182. Interview with Violet (Bottroff) McNett, by John Fritsche, May 23, 2010.
183. Interview and site visit with Louie Dalcerri, by John Fritsche, May 18, 2010.

CHAPTER 7

184. Kent Edward Haldan, *Our Japanese Citizens: A Study of Race, Class, and Ethnicity in Three Japanese American Communities in Santa Barbara County, 1900–1960* (PhD diss., University of California–Santa Barbara, 2000), 131.
185. Ibid., 131–33.
186. Ibid., 141.
187. *Los Angeles Times*, "Our Neighbors: A WEEKLY REVIEW OF AGRICULTURAL ACTIVITIES IN THE SOUTHWEST," April 5, 1931.
188. *Los Angeles Times*, "Which Cover Crop?: Cauliflower Growers Seek the Best for Their Conditions," February 14, 1932.
189. Haldan, *Our Japanese Citizens*, 144.
190. Ibid., 400.
191. Ibid., 164.
192. Hirahara, *An American Son*, 60.
193. Haldan, *Our Japanese Citizens*, 166.
194. Ibid., 167.

195. Iris Chang, *The Rape of Nanking: The Forgotten Holocaust of World War II* (Philadelphia, PA: Basic Books, 1997), 6.
196. Among several articles: *Los Angeles Times*, "Commander Hughes's Report on Bombing; Officer Graphically Describes Sinking of Panay and Flight of Survivors," December 25, 1937; *Los Angeles Times*, "Crisis Over Gunboat *Panay* at End, Declares Japan," December 27, 1937.
197. *Los Angeles Times*, "Plundering Japanese Rob Americans; Women and Children at Nanking Killed in Cold Blood," January 9, 1938.
198. Hallet Abend, "Terrors in Nanking Told; Japanese Declared Mistreating Hundreds of Women and Girls," *Los Angeles Times*, January 25, 1938.
199. Hirahara, *An American Son*, 61.
200. Ibid., 62.
201. Ibid., 75.
202. Ibid., 77.
203. Ibid., 77–78.
204. Haldan, *Our Japanese Citizens*, 417.
205. Hirahara, *An American Son*, 92.
206. Ibid., 93.
207. Haldan, *Our Japanese Citizens*, 402.
208. Ibid., 405.
209. Ibid., 427.
210. Hirahara, *An American Son*, 97–98.
211. Ibid., 105.
212. Ibid., 109.
213. Haldan, *Our Japanese Citizens*, 505.
214. E-mail from Karen Paaske to John Fritsche, June 14, 2010.
215. Haldan, *Our Japanese Citizens*, 525.
216. Ibid., 536.
217. *Los Angeles Times*, "'War Over' Judge Rules in Japanese Lease Suit," December 11, 1946.
218. *California Lettuce Growers, Inc. v. Union Sugar Company*, Supreme Court of California–Los Angeles, Case No. 23650 (1953).
219. G.A. Hancock Properties, Inc., "Captain Hancock," http://gahancockproperties.com/History_LP7A.html.
220. Norman Lowell McCarver Sr. and Norman Lowell McCarver Jr., *Hearne on the Brazos* (San Antonio: Century Press of Texas, 1958).
221. *Los Angeles Times*, "Hot Ice War Soon to Open: Precooling of Fruit Hard Blow to Producers," April 29, 1909.
222. E-mail exchange with Bruce Phillips, November 23, 2010.

Chapter 8

223. Wikipedia, "Blythe, California," http://en.wikipedia.org/wiki/Blythe,_California.
224. *Palo Verde Times*, "Blythe Ice Co to Build Ice Plant South of Town," January 22, 1942.
225. *Los Angeles Times*, "Fatal Auto Crash," August 17, 1926.
226. *Palo Verde Times*, "Blythe Ice Co to Build Ice Plant."
227. Interview with Pete Compten, March 2010.
228. *Palo Verde Times*, "New Plant, Blythe Ice Co., Under Construction," March 19, 1942.
229. "Blythe Ice Co Soon to Supply 100 Tons Daily," *Palo Verde Times*, June 11, 1942.
230. Blanche Copeland, e-mail, July 19, 2010.
231. *Palo Verde Times*, "Local Ice Co Negotiates $50K Refinancing Loan," September 24, 1942.
232. *Palo Verde Times*, "Valley's Biggest Vegetable Grower to Have 1,000 Acres," October 1, 1942.
233. *Palo Verde Times*, "Carrot Market Rosy Again," January 14, 1943.
234. *Palo Verde Times*, "Lettuce Carrot Markets Bring Cheer," January 21, 1943.
235. *Palo Verde Times*, "Big Canteloupe Season," February 18, 1943.
236. *Palo Verde Times*, "Melon Deal to Total 1205 Acres," April 15, 1943.
237. *Palo Verde Times*, "Comer Makes Cant Record," July 22, 1943.
238. *Palo Verde Times*, "Eaton Shed Destroyed by Fire," July 29, 1943.
239. *Palo Verde Times*, "Ca Veg Growers Plan Large Dev.," August 12, 1943.
240. *Palo Verde Times*, "Melon Deal to Total 1205 Acres," April 15, 1943.
241. *Palo Verde Times*, "30 Cars Lettuce Moved," December 23, 1943.
242. *Palo Verde Times*, "Melon Pack to Start Monday," June 10, 1943.
243. *Palo Verde Times*, "1943 Crops Worth $4.4M," January 28, 1944.
244. *Palo Verde Times*, "Lettuce by Air, from Blythe to New York City," December 27, 1945.
245. *Palo Verde Times*, "Don Dalzell Transferred to SB," February 28, 1946.
246. *Palo Verde Times*, "16 Million Pounds of Ice Used During June for Melon Crop," July 14, 1948.

Chapter 9

247. Interview with John Rasmussen, April 12, 2010.
248. Ibid., November 22, 2010.
249. Ibid., April 12, 2010.
250. Ibid., November 22, 2010.

About the Author

David Petry lives in Santa Barbara with his wife and three daughters. His journalism and historical work is focused on the evolution of institutions and the urban landscape. His published work includes a history of the Santa Barbara Cemetery, *The Best Last Place*, and an upcoming book covering the history of Cottage Health System in Santa Barbara County. Other work compiled on the site www.decomposingSB.com has included the history of alternate currencies, The Big Yellow House and neon in Santa Barbara.

Visit us at
www.historypress.net